W9-BSS-660

PRAISE FOR

ALL THE GOOD
IN SPORTS

Unfortunately, many of today's sports personalities are portrayed as being selfish and greedy. Not so with those you'll find in this book. They've chosen God first—not "me first."

Deb Patterson
Head Women's Basketball Coach
Kansas State University

This book is a very inspirational book that shares the stories and testimonies of some great athletes, who also share their faith and what it takes to be a champion on and off the field.

Gary Carter
Baseball Hall of Fame
Class of 2003

The men and women featured in this book have discovered a love that even their most adoring fans can't give them, and security that a guaranteed contract can't deliver. They're all role models.

Pat Williams
Author of *The Warrior Within*
Senior Vice President, Orlando Magic

Throughout the pages of this book, you will find athletes, coaches and broadcasters who have walked with the Lord, no matter what curveballs life has thrown them.

Dave Dravecky
Author of *Called Up: Stories of Life and Faith from the Great Game of Baseball*
Former major league pitcher, San Francisco Giants

Connecting the thrill of the game, the camaraderie of team and the excitement of individual achievement with powerful faith gives us a glimpse of what's to come and keeps our eye on the right ball!

Ryan Walter
Former hockey player
(15 NHL seasons, 1 Stanley Cup)
Adviser to the movie *Miracle*

Life is full of twists and turns that don't make sense. In these stories you will experience how these athletes have been able to overcome difficult challenges as they allowed God to move in their hearts and their lives.

Tracy Hanson
LPGA golfer

True Stories that Go Beyond the Headlines

ALL THE GOOD IN SPORTS

MIKE SANDROLINI
Sportswriter

Regal

From Gospel Light
Ventura, California, U.S.A.

Published by Regal Books
From Gospel Light
Ventura, California, U.S.A.

Library of Congress Cataloging-in-Publication Data
Sandrolini, Mike.
  All the good in sports : true stories that go beyond the headlines / Mike Sandrolini.
    p. cm.
  ISBN 978-0-8307-4474-9 (trade paper)
  1. Sports—Religious aspects. 2. Athletes—United States—Religious life. I. Title.
  GV706.42.S36 2007
  200'.88796—dc22

                                                                    2007011630

1 2 3 4 5 6 7 8 9 10 / 10 09 08 07

Rights for publishing this book in other languages are contracted by Gospel Light Worldwide, the international nonprofit ministry of Gospel Light. Gospel Light Worldwide also provides publishing and technical assistance to international publishers dedicated to producing Sunday School and Vacation Bible School curricula and books in the languages of the world. For additional information, visit www.gospellight worldwide.org; write to Gospel Light Worldwide, P.O. Box 3875, Ventura, CA 93006; or send an e-mail to info@gospellightworldwide.org.

To Ray and Donna Sandrolini.

It's only fitting that this book should be published around the time my parents celebrate their fiftieth wedding anniversary. I could write a book about their love, guidance and generosity. Thanks, Mom and Dad!

CONTENTS

FOREWORD

I developed a love and passion for the great game of baseball at an early age. That love and passion carried me through 19 major league seasons.

To be inducted into baseball's Hall of Fame made all the hard work and sacrifice worthwhile.

Certainly, I have missed the thrill of playing in front of large crowds, the competition and the fun of the game since retiring after the 1992 season. But faith and trust in the Lord have helped me face the reality of retirement and get on with life.

While I was writing my Hall of Fame induction speech, a great verse, Psalm 18, really spoke to me: "I love you, Lord; you are my strength. The Lord is my rock, my fortress, and my savior; my God is my rock, in whom I find protection. He is my shield, the power that saves me, and my place of safety. I called on the Lord, who is worthy of praise" (vv. 1-3, *NLT*).

The game of life through God makes each day a new challenge. There are always ups and downs. I have experienced the joys and blessings of a wonderful career filled with memories, and a wonderful family: my wife, Sandy; my daughters, Christy and Kim; and my son, D. J. I have also experienced the pain of losing my mother at a young age to leukemia, and my father passing away shortly after learning I had been voted into Cooperstown.

Yet the Lord has been with me through all of life's joys and sorrows, peaks and valleys. Those whom you will read about in this book have discovered that, too.

God bless!

Gary Carter
Inducted into the National Baseball Hall of Fame
in Cooperstown, NY, July 2003

INTRODUCTION

I began devouring the sports section at an early age. Mom and Dad subscribed to two newspapers back then—the same two they still get today: the *Chicago Tribune* and my hometown newspaper, the *Daily News-Tribune* in La Salle (for which I worked during college and after graduating from my alma mater, Illinois State University).

There was nothing fancy about the sports sections of yesteryear. No multicolor graphics, in-depth analysis of each play, digital photos, breakout boxes or quotes in large type. Just stories on games, box scores and black-and-white photos. Oftentimes, the photos were grainy, and newspapers would insert arrows within photos to point out, for example, the location of the ball or puck on a particular play.

I don't want to date myself too much, but we're talking between 30 and 40 years ago. It was a simpler, more innocent era, to be sure— an era during which I remember reading nothing but sports on the sports pages.

Times, of course, have changed. Some mornings, there's not much difference between the sports page and the front page. Or the *National Enquirer*. Or worse, the police blotter.

You can still find game stories nowadays, but more often than not, you also have to sift through accounts of athletes getting busted for drug possession; allegedly or actually using steroids; drinking too much; getting into scuffles at night clubs (or with fans or the media); having extramarital affairs; paying child support to a former girlfriend for their out-of-wedlock child; and my favorite, complaining about not getting any respect because one is not being paid "market value."

Who said there's no *I* in "team"?

However, we must keep in mind that the overwhelming majority of athletes, pro or otherwise, are good, kind, charitable people who strive to play by the rules. We just rarely hear about them because scandal, unfortunately, is what sells in our society.

Not anymore. In this book, we're going to push the malcontents, prima donnas and pouters in sports to the end of the line. The collection of stories from various authors contained in *All the Good in Sports* features men and women in the athletic arena who try to put their best foot forward each day. Some are superstars; others you might have never heard of. But whether or not they're well known, you'll discover the common denominator that drives them to succeed both on and off the field: their faith.

It's not as taboo as it once was for athletes to discuss their faith. Yet once the words "God," "Jesus," "the Lord" or "I'm a Christian" roll off their lips, they still tend to be dismissed as religious fanatics, holy rollers or Bible thumpers.

Sure, it's difficult not to be cynical when we hear about an athlete who is arrested and charged with soliciting a prostitute, and then learn he attended team chapel services every week. Or if you're like me, you begin to wonder if a batter who points to the sky after slugging a home run is just showboating for the cameras or really is giving kudos to the Big Guy.

A healthy degree of skepticism is fine. As someone who's been in the newspaper business for over 20 years—as well as in plenty of locker rooms—it's part of my job to be skeptical, question someone's motives and get to the heart of the matter.

The athletes, coaches and sports personalities in this book pull no punches. Sure, most of them have made millions of dollars. But to a man (or woman), they'll tell you they have found peace, purpose and security in their lives—the kind that can't be obtained by signing a 5-year contract with a $17 million bonus and a guaranteed motel suite on the road.

They see people in need around them, or around the world, and don't just talk about doing something. They take action to help meet those needs—not to gain notoriety or good press for themselves, but out of genuine love for others. And that love is rooted in their Christian faith.

You also won't find any holier-than-thou types in these pages. They ride life's roller coaster just like you and I. You'll meet some who have made bad choices, messed up big-time or struggled with addictions. Others have stared life-threatening situations in the face or have watched loved ones endure similar plights.

How have they overcome these aforementioned difficulties— some of which became full-blown crises? What do they do, and where do they turn, when faced with circumstances and tragedies that turn a life upside down and have no explanations or solutions? What motivates them to do the right or honorable thing, even though following through on their convictions might bring them more pain?

The choice of which stories to include was tough. I literally perused all of the issues of *Sports Spectrum* magazine dating back to the early 1990s in order to compile this collection. I then obtained the full cooperation of Robert Walker and the *Sports Spectrum* staff, and went about preparing the stories for this book. The stories you are about to read are adapted from the pages of *Sports Spectrum*, and I have had the distinct pleasure of writing an introduction for each one.

Please read on. I'm confident you'll learn what makes these good men and women of sports tick. I'm also confident you will be encouraged, inspired and uplifted by their stories. I know I have been.

Mike Sandrolini

ALL THE GOOD IN SPORTS

TONY DUNGY

WINNING SUPERBOWL COACH

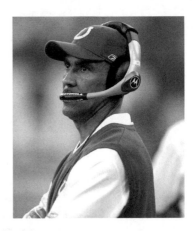

Moments after Tony Dungy's Indianapolis Colts had pounded the Chicago Bears 29-17 to win Super Bowl XLI, *CBS Sports'* Jim Nantz asked him about the significance of being the first African-American head coach to hoist the Lombardi Trophy. As always, Dungy was gracious and thoughtful, knowing exactly what to emphasize:

Nantz: This is one of those moments, Tony, where there is also social significance in this victory, and to have your hands on the Vince Lombardi Trophy. Tell me what this means to you right now.

Tony Dungy: I'll tell you what. I'm proud to be representing African-American coaches, to be the first African-American to win this. It means an awful lot to our country. But again, more than anything, I've said it before, Lovie Smith [the Bears's coach] and I, [are] not only the first two African-Americans, but Christian coaches, showing that you can win doing it the Lord's way. And we're more proud of that.

Few coaches can rival Dungy's success in the National Football League. Legendary names such as Vince Lombardi, Tom Landry, Don Shula and Joe Gibbs come to mind—but not many others. Dungy's Colts have won 10 or more games in each season of his 5-year tenure. Add to that his prior success leading the Tampa Bay Buccaneers, and Dungy is now just the thirty-fifth coach in NFL history to win 100 games. He is only the third person to win a Super

Bowl as both a player and a coach—he collected a ring with the Pittsburgh Steelers' championship team in 1978.

Yet success has been bittersweet for Dungy. Tragedy struck him and his wife, Lauren, in late December 2005, when their 18-year-old son James was discovered dead in his Florida apartment. He had apparently taken his own life—the cruelest of blows for any parent. Dungy eventually returned to coaching, and he credits his Christian faith with helping him cope, despite admitting months later, "It's still very, very painful."

Dungy later told ESPN's Michael Smith, "I've said all along that God is in control. I have to believe that He's in control here, too."

The following article was written about Tony Dungy before his son's death, and before his Super Bowl win.

QUIET FIRE

By Ted Kluck

The fire in Tony Dungy's spirit doesn't come out in screaming and ranting but in determined, strong, intelligent leadership— and his method seems to work.

Tony Dungy's gimmick is not having a gimmick.

After a decade that made antiheroes cliché (the 1990s), Dungy's single most rebellious act may be the fact that he flies under the radar and lives quietly. While Jon Gruden is the young screamer, Mike Martz is the tormented genius, and Tom Coughlin is just tormented, Tony Dungy is, well, just Tony Dungy.

And on this particular day during summer training camp, 2005, he's hard to track down. It's 8:45 A.M. on a hot morning in Terre Haute, a city that's not really known for anything besides being voted (oddly, along with Dungy's childhood home Jackson,

Michigan) as one of the most unremarkable cities in the United States. It is, however, home to the Rose-Hulman Institute of Technology, summer residence of the Indianapolis Colts.

In today's NFL, training camp has become a largely symbolic exercise. With minicamps, quarterback schools, "voluntary" work-outs and OTAs (organized team activities), the team is on-site year-round and training camp has become an unnecessary relic. But the Colts are one of a handful of NFL teams that still pack it up and make the trek from their multimillion-dollar practice facility in Indianapolis to a small college 30 miles away, where players live and eat in dormitories designed not for 300-pound athletes but for 160-pound engineering students.

On this day, Dungy is moving quietly from practice group to practice group on a field that is eerily quiet. There is very little banter and no yelling—an atmosphere that suggests that his team is all business. Dungy wields the master whistle, and on his chirp the team moves from station to station. There are no air-horns and no intricate on-field clocks. Even running back Edgerrin James, he of the long dreadlocks, moves with an air of maturity. He does everything his coach asks of him, and he puts on a clinic in a one-on-one pass rush drill, stonewalling every linebacker placed in front of him—the distinct pop of plastic on plastic the only sound filling the air. Starters are starters for a reason.

On the other side of the ball, Gary Brackett, all 5' 10" of him, barrels into fullbacks and tight ends from his starting middle line-backer position, leapfrogging over former first-round pick Rob Morris.

Brackett, who went undrafted after a college career at Rutgers, considers Dungy a father figure. "I lost my father, mother and one brother all within my first two years in the league, so it's been a tough couple of years for me," he says. "Tony Dungy has been like a father figure. He's consistent. He played in the league, so he knows how it is to be a player. He's a humble, no-nonsense kind of guy."

Brackett is the kind of guy most teams try very hard to replace. He is the smallest player in his position group. Even his impeccably tailored NFL uniform hangs awkwardly off his short legs. But, as the cliché goes, he just makes plays.

"Coach Dungy gave me an opportunity. Nobody else gave me a chance to make this team, and I've just hung around and persevered. Every day is a test of my faith because the NFL is full of spiritual challenges. But now I'm being rewarded for my hard work," says Brackett.

Coach Dungy is extremely down to earth, and he approaches each player as a man. The most surprising thing is that when a player makes a mistake, he almost feels like he is letting Dungy down personally. He has been called the most boring man in professional football. He is in charge of a supposedly passionless quarterback who throws for 40 touchdowns a season, and his team has "no identity" but scores 40 points a game, even though his best running back didn't want to be there.

Dungy spends a good deal of the practice alone, and when he finds me afterward he walks toward me by himself, not surrounded by the usual heel-nipping entourage that most public figures carry with them. I tell him about Brackett's father-figure comment. Dungy laughs. Humility is the ability to be a father figure and not know it.

"I remember when I came into the league as a coach at age 25, I used to be a brother figure! The dynamic changes," he says, "when you are in charge of 53 guys instead of just a handful. But I still enjoy seeing guys improve on and off the field.

"Gary Brackett has perseverance. He went from unheralded to a really good player. That seems to be his M.O. in this league."

For a while, Tony Dungy was known only as the "black head-coaching candidate." He was the guy the networks would cut to with a headset on in the booth, saying for years that he would be a suitable candidate for an NFL coaching job. But the offers never came, and while others such as Rich Kotite, Joe Bugel and Art Shell got their second chances, Dungy waited.

The city of Indianapolis suits Dungy. It is under the NFL radar, and its fans are Midwesterners in search of something to do rather than battery-and-epithet throwing East Coasters. The Colts have embraced them, and the gamble seems to be working. The stands are full this morning and there seems to be nary a fan without a piece of officially licensed NFL blue-and-white apparel.

"Most of our guys are hard-working types," says Dungy. "We have a few stars, but by and large we have a lot of role players."

Coming from Jackson, Michigan, one can't help but be humble. It was once voted the worst city in the United States and boasts only a state prison and a few chain restaurants to go with crumbling houses and a struggling economy. This is where Dungy cut his teeth. He excelled as a high school quarterback and found his way to the University of Minnesota. Dungy graduated with a bachelor's degree in business administration and signed as a free agent with the Steelers in May 1977. He was converted from quarterback to wide receiver to safety, and when he made the team, he was the first free agent to make the Steelers' final roster in two seasons.

After a brief NFL career, Dungy went into coaching. And, like most other coaches, he hit the road, with stops at the University of Minnesota (defensive backs) and then Pittsburgh, Kansas City and Minnesota as a defensive coordinator.

"God has expectations of you in this business. You're a lamp and how you carry yourself is very important in the midst of the spiritual challenges."

What challenges?

"Remaining humble when you do well, and keeping a decent attitude when you're losing. You get the sense in this league that not everyone can end up the big winner. At the end of a season you have to evaluate the spiritual side of what you accomplish."

Dungy is refreshingly honest.

"It's actually easier to stay locked in spiritually during the seasons," Dungy says. "You know it's going to be tough, and you prepare for it. You build in a little bit of extra time in the morning to read, and we have some neat Christian guys on our staff to stay accountable."

Former Colts return man Troy Walters talks about Dungy's reliability, how he is the same person on and off the field. Dungy picked Walters off the NFL's waiver wire after he was released by Minnesota in 2002. I ask Walters about the team's identity.

"We don't really have one," he says after some thought. "We just don't get too high or too low and take care of our business."

The Colts, both Christians and otherwise, keep a low profile, choosing instead to simply "bang somebody up" and take care of their business on the field. In a league of chest thumps and fingers pointed toward the sky—where even faith is a commodity—less is more on this team. As far as coach Tony Dungy is concerned, that's just fine.

ALBERT PUJOLS

WORLD SERIES CHAMPION

Albert Pujols is the leading cause of insomnia in major league baseball. Who knows how many opposing pitchers and managers have spent sleepless nights trying to figure out how to pitch to such a devastating hitter. To a man, they will likely tell you—*it's an exercise in futility!*

Pujols has been a pitcher's worst dream ever since he broke into the major leagues with the St. Louis Cardinals in 2001. Winning Rookie of the Year honors that season proved to be just the tip of the iceberg for Pujols, who has since rocketed to superstardom and is now considered baseball's most feared—and productive—hitter.

In a sport rich with legends and steeped in tradition, no other player in baseball history has equaled Pujols's .300-plus batting average, his more than 30 home runs, over 100 runs batted in and his 100-plus runs in each of his first 6 years. After finishing second to Barry Bonds as the National League MVP in both the 2002 and 2003 seasons, Pujols won the coveted MVP award in 2005, hitting .330 with 41 homers and 117 RBIs.

In 2006, the Cardinals' first baseman put together another monster season, achieving single-season career highs in home runs (49) and RBIs (137). He slugged a major-league record 14 home runs for the month of April and won his first Gold Glove. More important, he helped lead the Cardinals to their first World Series championship since 1982.

Pujols is an MVP off the field as well. After their daughter Isabella was born with Down syndrome in 2005, Pujols and his wife, Deidre, established the Pujols Family Foundation. This nonprofit organization is dedicated to caring for kids with Down syndrome both in the United States and abroad, as well as helping poor children in the Dominican Republic, where Pujols was born.

IT'S IN THE CARDS

By Allen Palmeri and Lee Warren

Led by Albert Pujols, the St. Louis Cardinals have plenty of talent and an unmistakable added dimension.

Gruesomely cool images of St. Louis Cardinals' first baseman Albert Pujols dance into your living room like a Dominican Republic merengue.

Pujols wears a warrior mask as he menacingly swings his bat to the rhythm that Nike dictates. The Cardinals' superstar—the cornerstone of the new Busch Stadium, which opened in 2006—is a commercial success.

Pujols has come a long way from just a few seasons ago when he first suited up in the Cards's famous double-birded home jersey.

"I remember 2001 when I first made the team," he says. "I was really scared because I was a young Christian, and I didn't know how things were going to go until one of the best teammates I had, Mike Matheny, took me under his wing and told me everything was going to be all right."

"I'm pretty sure it was the same way with Stan Musial. When he played, they tried to take care of each other and help each other out."

Stan Musial is synonymous with baseball history in St. Louis. And for many observers, Pujols's talent calls to mind the greatness of Stan the Man.

Clearly, part of the secret within Albert Pujols is the secret of the storied St. Louis Cardinals franchise, a National League fixture since 1892 and winner of 10 world championships. Pujols is standing on the shoulders of such Cardinal Hall of Famers as Musial, Enos "Country" Slaughter, Dizzy Dean, Lou Brock, Bob Gibson and Ozzie Smith.

Pujols understands the pull baseball has with the fans in what some call the best baseball city in the land.

"It's awesome to see 35,000 to 45,000 people every night," says the slugger, who went to high school in Independence, Missouri. "When you see a 65- or 75-year-old person with a lineup card, and he is writing down everything you do, it's unbelievable. You don't see that in every stadium.

"I think that goes with the respect the guys from the past have built up. That's why I say Lou Brock, Red Schoendienst and the rest of those guys put the city of St. Louis where [it is]. A lot of people know that the Cardinals fans are the best. I'm glad the Lord put me in this city."

Pujols knows that there is more in St. Louis these days than standing on the shoulders of past Cardinal greats. He is also standing shoulder to shoulder in a different way with Cardinal teammates.

Together, these Christian athletes have one goal: to represent the great St. Louis Cardinals baseball tradition in a way that will glorify God. Pujols needs the support of those guys, for, as he says, "I'm still a baby in Christ. I keep learning and just follow my leader—follow the things that the Lord wants me to do."

Cody McKay, a former backup catcher with the Cardinals, understands the dual responsibility of Cardinal history and Christian commitment.

"We need to give back as much as they give to us, for the Kingdom, to make Jesus famous in St. Louis," McKay says.

Back in 1991, Jesus was hardly famous among the Cardinals. When a Cardinals fan named Judy Boen stepped out in faith to launch the first Christian Family Day at an American sports stadium, she sensed that players were afraid to testify for Christ.

It took a rather unknown pitcher named Scott Terry, who raced onto the field with his glove as visual aid to share the gospel, to plant the seed. Christian Family Day has since blossomed into a multi-state draw for the Cardinals—to the tune of 12,000 tickets. Several other professional teams in various sports venues now have similar events.

Part of the ongoing legacy of Christian Family Day in St. Louis is that a player like Pujols can speak freely about his relationship with Christ within a greater clubhouse culture that continues to be penetrated by light. When pitcher Andy Benes came to the Cardinals in 1996, both he and his wife, Jennifer, noted at the time how easy it was to speak about spiritual things because of the pioneering work of Boen and her Christian Family Day committee members.

Boen's daughter, Christe, is a chiropractor whose patients have included Pujols and a few other Cardinals players. Several years ago, she came up with the idea to make baseball cards with testimonies from the Cardinals.

Deidre Pujols, Albert's wife, says these cards have provided great protection from overzealous fans. "They think they're just getting a baseball card and an autograph until they really read what's on the back of it," she says. "It's all about Albert's testimony, and it's so awesome to have that because I believe that card helps take away that superstar [status]."

Christe Boen estimates that more than 1 million of these Christian baseball cards have been handed out over the last few years, with more than 50,000 alone being distributed at the 2004 Christian Family Day.

"When Albert handed them out in the Dominican [Republic], he stopped traffic one day because everyone was trying to get one when they recognized him," she says.

Pujols and the Boens worship together at West County Community Church, in the St. Louis suburb of Wildwood, where Phil Hunter is the pastor. Hunter's zeal for evangelism has born fruit in the St. Louis professional sports community through athletes like Pujols who feel comfortable letting him into their circle of confidants.

For the Cardinals slugger, Hunter developed a special A-to-Z list on the attributes of Jesus. Pujols is in the process of using this list to brag on Jesus among his teammates.

This A-to-Z list consists of character qualities such as "Almighty," "Beautiful" and "Comforter." Hunter explains that as the believer shares his faith through this method, he lifts up Jesus in evangelism so that all people will be drawn to Him (see John 12:32).

Hunter and Boen both have noticed Pujols taking this seriously, and it has greatly encouraged them. Boen says she is thankful she can count on him to support her in the days leading up to Christian Family Day, knowing that the Cardinals leader and his wife both have a desire to magnify Christ.

"Deidre and Albert get what we're trying to accomplish," Boen says.

Three young men from the church like to play video games with Pujols. These are Hunter's sons—Phil Jr., Joshua and Matt. The youngest brother says they all act like family.

"Everybody always treats Albert like he's something special, and we just treat him like he's one of us," Matt Hunter says. "He's just another guy. Everybody needs encouragement, and everybody needs prayer. My dad has really discipled Albert, and the three of us all kind of have our own different roles. We come alongside Albert and love him not because he's a baseball player but because he's God's child, and God is using him to advance the Kingdom. We just are brothers with him."

In recent years, the Cardinals have been blessed with a strong group of Christians, such as Matheny, Woody Williams, Cal Eldred, Reggie Sanders and So Taguchi—all of whom were part of the 2004 Cardinals World Series team along with Pujols, all of whom have been part of a tapestry that runs red with the color of the Cardinals as well as with the redeeming blood of Christ.

Matheny, Williams, Eldred and Sanders are no longer with the team, but relief pitchers Braden Looper and Adam Wainwright, catcher Yadier Molina and starting pitcher Kip Wells have since joined Pujols and Taguchi in the Cardinals' dugout, giving the Redbirds a solid core of believers. Christian TV and radio announcers like Wayne Hagin and Rick Horton add to the Master's work of art along the Gateway Arch.

So what happens when these Cardinal players get together—away from the pressures of the game and immersed in Christian fellowship?

"We encourage each other," Pujols says. "We have a prayer time. We also have a Bible study on Sunday, which is awesome. We have a great study time every Wednesday.

"I remember a couple of years ago, we were reading a book, *The Purpose-Driven Life*, and we would get together on road trips. We'd have 12 or 13 guys in the room after a night game. We didn't care [how late it was], because if you don't have time for the Lord, you don't have time for anything."

Some of these guys also eagerly step out into the spotlight to testify during Christian Family Day. During the summer of 2004—in what may have been the most powerful testimony for the King of kings ever communicated at Busch Stadium—a group of four Cardinals players and one coach came onto the field at Christian Family Day to gather around a 14-foot replica of a Roman cross built right there at the ballpark by evangelist Joe White.

Pujols, Matheny, Taguchi and Eldred (Cal retired from baseball after the 2005 season) stood with first base coach Dave McKay, Cody's father, as White, founder of Kanakuk Kamps in Branson, Missouri, explained how the cross would remain a constant in history after all of their athletic fame is gone.

"It's safe to say it's a Christian-based ball club," Cody McKay says. "If you ever have a question, there's somebody to go to, and we're there for each other. I've come from different teams where it's just not there."

Following the 2004 season, Matheny told Pujols it was his turn to be the spiritual leader of the Cardinals.

"Well, that's my job," says Pujols, laughing. "He told me to keep growing and to come as a leader and take care of the young guys coming up."

Part of his overall leadership emphasis is to play the game the way Musial, Brock and Gibson played it—with a great deal of respect for the Cardinal name and tradition.

"They played the game hard," Pujols says. "As young players right now, that's the same thing we want to do."

Horton, who pitched for the 1985 and 1987 Cardinals teams that won the National League pennant, says that Cardinals fans tend to act like folks from a small town cheering for their local high school baseball team.

"I know from my travels that it's not the same in other places," Horton says. "St. Louis is not a college town. It's really a baseball town—a Cardinal town in terms of its identity. I think the players really reap the rewards from that because you get a different kind of connection here with the fans.

"For six months you are what's happening. You're on the front page of the sports section and you are what people talk about at the water coolers at work. You drive around town and you see people wearing red. In pennant races, everybody wears red. It's kind of humbling, in a way, because you realize you're a part of the psyche of an entire city."

Now, even more of the attention is being focused on Pujols—not simply for his hitting and fielding, but also for his walk with the Lord Jesus Christ. That's fine with the young superstar.

"I think there are some people who look at me and say, 'Oh, man, you are awesome.' They look at me like that and I say, 'Hey, I'm trying to follow my Lord Jesus.' That's who I'm trying to represent every day I step on the field."

McKay sees the shift in leadership to Pujols as a positive. Cardinal players will follow this merengue.

"I think Albert takes it to a different level where his relationship with God is evident throughout the league, with his teammates and at home," McKay says.

RUTH RILEY

WNBA SUPERSTAR

Notre Dame Fighting Irish lore is rich with legends such as Knute Rockne, Paul Hornung, Joe Montana and Jerome Bettis. However, no listing of Notre Dame greats would be complete without the name Ruth Riley.

Riley is the *only* women's basketball player in Notre Dame history to tally 2,000 points and 1,000 rebounds during her career. But no year topped 2001, when she led the Fighting Irish to the national championship. Among her honors that year, she was named Most Valuable Player of the NCAA Division I Final Four, won the Naismith Player of the Year award and was named the Associated Press Player of the Year.

Riley then brought her considerable talents into the professional ranks, where she became the fifth overall selection in the 2001 WNBA draft. After spending two seasons with the soon-to-be-defunct Miami Sol, Riley became the Detroit Shock's No. 1 pick in the 2003 WNBA Dispersal Draft. With Detroit, she promptly helped the Shock win the league's championship crown by beating the two-time defending champions, the Los Angeles Sparks. The 6' 5" center pumped in 27 points during the championship clincher and was named the Finals' MVP. Riley and the Shock took home even more WNBA championship hardware in 2006 as they beat the Sacramento Monarchs in five games for the title.

Success seems to follow Riley, who displayed her championship ways while representing America as a member of the U.S. team that took silver at the 1999 World University Games, and as part of the gold medal 2004 U.S. Olympic team.

ESPN named Riley one of women's college basketball's top 25 players of the past 25 years. Her accomplishments are not limited to the basketball court, either, as she has been recognized by the WNBA for her participation in the Detroit Shock's community service programs. She is also involved in organizations such as Athletes in Action, Orchards Children's Services (a child-welfare agency that cares for homeless children in Southeast Lower Michigan), the March of Dimes and the American Cancer Society.

Ruth Riley joins the grand tradition of "Golden Domers" who have made their names legendary in the world of professional athletics, yet sports is not all Ruth Riley is about—in fact, it's not even what she's *primarily* about. Riley is first and foremost a woman of faith, and she doesn't back away from the challenges that come from seeking to follow Christ while pursuing her athletic dreams.

THE LIFE OF RILEY

By Dave Branon

On April 2, 2001, Ruth Riley and her teammates at Notre Dame inspired a nation with their selfless play as they captured the school's first NCAA women's basketball national championship. Riley, the Naismith Player of the Year, was remarkable—scoring 28 points on 9-of-13 shooting and 10 free throws—in leading the Irish past Purdue 68-66. Riley went on to play for two years with the Miami Sol in the WNBA and spent the off-season before the 2003 WNBA year playing in Spain. That April, the Detroit Shock of the WNBA picked Riley in the Dispersal Draft of players from two failed WNBA teams.

Sports Spectrum: Talk about the town of Macy, Indiana, where you grew up.

Ruth Riley: Macy is your typical small Indiana town. It boasts approximately 380 people, has a few stop signs, two churches, and an obligatory post office. The people live the simple, quiet lives that are associated with the surrounding farming community. Over the years I have heard many jokes about my hometown, but I love it. I love the fact that life is slower and more relaxed, many people today still don't lock their doors at night, and you wave to everyone you pass on the country dirt roads because the odds of not knowing that person are very slim.

Sports Spectrum: You grew up in a single-parent home as the middle child. What did your mom do to provide for you and your siblings?

Riley: We moved more times than I can count on both hands, but most of my life was spent living on a farm. For the most part we never did the actual farming ourselves. My mom was a single parent raising my older sister, Rachel, younger brother, Jacob, and myself. Mom always found a way to provide us with the basics. We knew what it was like to go without a lot of things, but we didn't mind because we were going without together. Going without worldly resources caused us to be more creative in how we approached things, and I also learned the reward of hard work—and the sense of accomplishment that came along with it.

Sports Spectrum: What are some of the core values and lessons your mom taught you?

Riley: My mom started off as a beautician, working in a shop adjacent to our house—this enabled her to be an active part of our lives. It was important to her to be there to raise us, and I'm grateful that she was always around. I grew up attending church, and my mom emphasized Christian morals and values in us kids. I was raised with a solid understanding of what is right and wrong. Respect was something Mom demanded of us, and it has had a lasting effect on my life. Respecting my elders, teachers, peers and respecting differences: cultures, environments and opinions.

Sports Spectrum: How did you cope with being tall, and how did your mom help you with it?

Riley: Many people ask me if I have always been tall, and to that I answer emphatically "Yes!" My sister and I were the same height when I was 18 months old and she was 3. Unfortunately, I haven't always handled my height so well. "Sit up straight" and "Walk proud" were constant instructions from my mother. For children, anything out of the ordinary is subject to criticism, and I found a lot of it thrown my way. Self-confidence was something I definitely lacked; therefore, my personality was a lot more withdrawn than it is today. I was extremely shy and opened up only to those I felt comfortable around. Athletics became my way of escape, and through basketball I found my acceptance. I grew up as one of the boys, and I loved it.

Sports Spectrum: What was life like for you at North Miami High School?

Riley: Through the combination of my mom emphasizing academics and [my] being extremely competitive in nature, I was able to excel in school as well as have athletic success. I moved from a very large junior high school in Grove City, Ohio, where I was definitely not an impact player (second and third string) to my tiny high school (83 in my graduating class). As the tallest girl in the school, I found myself the starting center by default. A college scholarship was something I had always dreamed about, but not something I thought would be a reality until I started receiving recruiting letters. Soon I found myself in the complex process of college recruiting. I received letters from every major U.S. university, and I was facing one of the biggest decisions of my life. My mom was there for support, but the decision was mine. Notre Dame was always at the top of my list and the only place I went to visit before I signed.

Sports Spectrum: Were you able to maintain a normal life at Notre Dame while pursuing your studies and basketball?

Riley: The transition to college was a hard one for me. College athletics are demanding, and time management proves to be one of the most important lessons to learn as a freshman. I suddenly found myself training twice as much as I had been used to, taking classes more intense than I had ever seen, and trying in my shy way to meet new people and fit in socially.

Everyone adjusts differently, and a lot of that has to do with personality and what a person wants to achieve. I knew what I wanted, and I knew it would mean a lot of sacrifices, but I was willing to make them. Was I able to be a "normal student" and play college basketball? No, but that isn't something I feel I missed. It's a trade-off. Although I missed out on a lot of social events most students were able to do, I also experienced a lot through basketball they weren't able to. I put my social life on the shelf my first few years at Notre Dame. I was more interested in getting good grades and improving on the court.

As a young player, you think sacrifice is the only way to success, but as I have gotten older I realize sacrifice is essential, but there has to be a balance to it. My senior year I finally found the balance I needed, and I wouldn't trade those memories for anything. I left my college career with an amazing education from a university I learned to love, the highest level of success achievable on the collegiate level, and friends and acquaintances for a lifetime. I have been blessed!

It was at college where my relationship with the Lord began to grow. When you are on your own and forced to make decisions for yourself—your faith and beliefs are tested, and tested a lot in an intellectual environment. I had a great foundation in Jesus Christ, but it was more of the faith of a child—simple, blind faith. My later years at Notre Dame, I found a great group of fellow Christian athletes—older ones I could look up to. Athletics are very demanding of your time, and you really have to be careful that it doesn't affect your priorities. Faith, family, school and basketball were always the order I professed concerning my priorities, and I found that my faith and family were sacrificed a lot in the early years.

Sports Spectrum: Your senior year at Notre Dame must seem like a storybook year. As you review that remarkable season, what stands out?

Riley: There were numerous highlights of my senior year. On the court would definitely be winning a national championship. We had a special class of five seniors who had gone through so much together—it was a perfect end to our collegiate career. Off the court would have to be graduation day. My sister, Rachel, and I graduated together, and it was such an emotional day to experience with all my friends and family.

Sports Spectrum: Can you talk about when you trusted Christ as your Savior and what has prompted your growth as a believer?

Riley: A lot of people know exactly to the day when they gave their life to Christ. I do not have that information. I grew up in church, always believed what I had learned, and I know that I trusted Jesus as my personal Savior when I was young. The significance of my relationship with Him is what changed over the years. Once I got to college, I started to intellectually understand what my heart already knew. During my two years with the Miami Sol in the WNBA, I grew an amazing amount, and in my time over in Spain even more so.

With every life change comes an adjustment, and that was definitely true for my rookie season in the WNBA. For the first time I found myself a long, long way from home. I was homesick at first and trying to live up to the expectations of their top draft pick.

I was fortunate to have some Christian teammates and a Christian assistant coach. One of my favorite things about the WNBA is the fact that every team has a designated chaplain and chapel service before the game. Arlene DeBardelaben proved to be my spiritual mentor, and I am so blessed for that. Everyone should have someone they trust and can come to with questions or for guidance.

For the first time in my life I had time to read and study the materials I chose to—not more classes or required reading. Before then I sadly admit my devotion to God's Word on a regular basis was very poor. Arlene provided me with books and tapes that aided in my spiritual growth. Although I was now immersed in the life of professional athletics, which is not exactly a godly atmosphere, I found myself growing more than I ever had before.

One strong test of my faith came after I had trained in Miami for the entire off-season, and the day before our first game I found that I had broken my little finger on my shooting hand. I had never before had an injury that kept me from playing this sport, and it was definitely a test of patience and character. The whole season proved to be a struggle and ended with the knowledge that the Sol would no longer be a franchise in the WNBA. Oddly enough, this did not bother me—I had confidence that where I would be next would be part of God's plan. So now I'm in Detroit!

During my season in Spain, I played in Valencia, Spain, for a team called Ros Casares. We lost in the Euroleague playoffs, won the Spanish Cup, and made it to the finals of the Spanish league. Basketball-wise this was really what I needed. I needed a healthy season to just play and get back in the flow and get my confidence back after an injury-filled WNBA season.

I can honestly say that my relationship with God grew the most while I was in Spain. One of the first things you will notice in Spain is the lack of Christianity. Although most of the country is Catholic, I would say this is true of mostly the older generations. I came equipped with many books to read, and Arlene sent me tapes to listen to. I also received tapes from my church back in Miami (Calvary Chapel). My Spanish has improved, and I was blessed to find fellowship at a local church where two American missionaries had found a home. Two amazing workbooks, *Experiencing God* and *The Purpose Driven Life*, helped me immensely.

Sports Spectrum: What is hard about being young in this society and trying to live for Jesus all the time?

Riley: Every day is a challenge, whether you are 23 or 63, to live a life for Christ. He made a point in telling us that following Him is not going to be easy in this world. Many people in their early 20s are on their own, pursuing success on worldly terms, and not really focused on their faith. Many people I have come into contact with believe in God but see religion as something they will "start practicing" once they get older.

Everyone has this innate desire to be accepted, and that sometimes keeps me from vocalizing my faith, because of fear of rejection from my peers. This is something I am constantly working on. The challenges I find are being unafraid to be open about my faith, especially with my semi-reserved personality. This is an area I have improved a lot in, but I still have a long way to go. Basketball has provided me with a platform, which means my life is under constant scrutiny. I find one of the biggest challenges is living what I believe—this is a challenge we all face every day.

DWIGHT HOWARD

RISING NBA STAR

The No. 1 overall pick in the 2004 NBA draft had never stepped onto a collegiate basketball court in his life. He was Dwight Howard, from a tiny, private prep school called Southwest Atlanta Christian Academy. Howard had one simple goal: to be the best player in basketball. He had a good start, too; he was the winner of the 2003-2004 Naismith Award, given only to the nation's best high school player.

Howard wasn't the first prep star to leap straight to the pros. Kevin Garnett, Kobe Bryant and LeBron James had each made the jump to pro basketball right after high school graduation day. But in his rookie season, the 6' 11" forward accomplished what no other prep-to-pro phenom had: He started every single game.

Howard didn't merely play during his rookie year; he also set an NBA record by becoming the youngest player in league history to pull down 20 or more rebounds in a single game. Not only that, but he also averaged a double-double (double figures in points and in rebounds) for the year—the youngest player in NBA history to ever do so. Along the way, he led the Orlando Magic in rebounding, in field goal percentage and in shots blocked.

Howard is accumulating accolades for his off-court work, as well. The Orlando Magic Youth Foundation awarded him with the 2004-2005 Rich and Helen DeVos Community Enrichment Award, given annually to the Magic player whose efforts enhance other people's lives. Also in 2004, he started the Dwight Howard Foundation, which provides students with scholarships to attend Southwest Atlanta Christian Academy.

As part of the 2007 NBA All-Star festivities in Las Vegas, a slam-dunk contest was held. Dwight Howard participated and awed fans with a super slam in his first attempt. The judges gave him high marks. On his second slam, Howard dunked the ball with one hand—at first glance a rather unspectacular performance. The announcers were the first to notice that with Howard's non-dunking hand, he had slapped a sticker on the highest point of the face of the backboard. Replays showed that the sticker featured a photo of Howard. A closer look revealed that Howard had written on the sticker "All Things Through Christ: Phil 4:13," referring to Philippians 4:13. After the game, Orlando Magic vice president Pat Williams thanked Howard for his witness, but noted that while everyone saw the sticker, most missed the Bible reference. "That's okay," Howard told Williams. "God saw it."

THE DWIGHT STUFF

By Victor Lee

*Two Dwights make a right as dad and son work together to make
sure Dwight Howard's NBA experience is a success.*

It was Dwight Howard's birthday.

He was six months away from being a trazillionaire. He was a blimp—not a blip—on the NBA draft radar. The next high school phenom-turned-pro superstar. The first pick among the first picks. The Future.

So did Daddy go borrow against future earnings and deliver a Hummer? Did he get a PDA with built-in phone, headphones, MP3 player and hot chick-finding radar?

No. He got an alarm clock.

An alarm clock.

Such is the sobering world of the 18-year-old who has it all—but hasn't taken delivery yet. You see, Dwight wants to deliver first. Kind of an old-school mind-set. It's an others-first thing. A matter of integrity. A righteous pride.

It's what got him up at 5 A.M. (that's why he needed the alarm clock) to shoot baskets in an empty high school gymnasium when he could have been sleeping in, waiting for the draft, dreaming about the Brinks truck about to back up to his door and deliver green goodies.

You see, Dwight Howard does not yet believe the world revolves around him, and if anybody tells him otherwise, they'll have his state-trooper daddy, Orlando Magic senior vice president Pat Williams, and a few others to deal with.

Dwight Howard: real talented, real grounded. Just plain real.

Who Is This Guy?

A successful life is best begun with sound upbringing and continues by accurately defining who you are. Natural ability, intellectual inclination and passion of the heart combine with spiritual beliefs to create a profile of a person.

In a Christian context, understanding who God made you to be is crucial. Operate outside of that identity, and failure is likely while dissatisfaction is virtually assured. Operate within, and God's power flows through the purposes He gave you to accomplish. Deep satisfaction usually follows. This simple-but-profound theology is important when considering Dwight Howard Jr.

"Dwight Howard is a fun-loving, easy-going type of kid," says Dwight, referring to himself in the third person, something one might be tempted to do when life—even one as carefully scripted and anticipated as his has been—suddenly takes on attributes of fame and fortune one can hardly imagine. "I like to have a lot of fun, but I know when it's time to get serious. I like everybody being happy and peaceful. And by the end of the day, by people being around me so long, they'll see God in me. That's the beauty of being a good Christian. Just live it, and He'll come through."

Just living the Christian life is what the Howard family has been doing throughout Dwight's upbringing. Dwight comes from a working-class family in a middle-class, mid-South city. He attended a small private school that would be considered cloistered by the irreligious but focused by the faithful. Mom is a physical education teacher and former basketball player on the first Morris Brown

College women's team. Dwight Sr. is a state trooper and athletic director of the tiny (16 in Dwight's graduating class) Southwest Atlanta Christian Academy.

"Basically, since I was a young kid, I just talk to God every day," Dwight Jr. says. "I thank Him for everything He's done. I thank Him for the little things. God has done so much—I just thank Him dearly. That keeps me aware that God is always going to be with me. He's never going to leave me, no matter what I do in life. That knowledge is what makes me strong in Him."

That knowledge is modeled by Mom and Dad to Dwight and his two siblings (he's the middle child). They appreciate what is happening to their family, because they've worked hard for what they have and they have suffered through heartaches. They chose to make financial sacrifices in order to send their children to a Christian school. They suffered through the agony of the miscarriages of seven other children before Dwight was born.

It's a focused family, a group that believes what happens to them externally can't change who they are internally. Nobody is complaining about the influx of a few million dollars, but no one is changing character either.

"Things in the family are pretty much the same," Dwight Sr. says as he sits in Orlando (where the family was building a home) in Dwight Jr.'s apartment a few weeks before his first pro training camp. "We did receive a lot of publicity last year [Dwight's senior year in high school], but I think everybody stayed on an even keel. Dwight stayed humble.

"We often remind ourselves, 'This is God [doing this].' My wife and I were talking about . . . how a few months ago we were a state trooper and a school teacher, and things changed so rapidly. But it's just by the grace of God, and we need to put that on the forefront. This entire journey is a blessing of God.

"We're living one day at a time and not getting overwhelmed."

The even keel that steadies Dwight Howard Jr. was exposed a few years ago when it became obvious that Dwight's talent would take him at least to the major college level. Back then, to go for the glory at all costs might have meant moving Dwight to a public school—a bigger arena with a bigger window through which the world could watch Dwight.

"We thought about it [when Dwight was] in the eighth grade," Dwight Sr. says. "We had been in a Christian athletic association not sanctioned by the state. We'd been approached since the sixth grade about putting him in bigger schools. Even AAU coaches were saying, 'You've got him at the wrong school; he won't be exposed.'

"We told them we believed God that whoever needed to see him would see him."

Under Howard's leadership as athletic director, Southwestern Atlanta Christian Academy upgraded its program. It played some elite teams during Dwight Jr.'s years there.

"We went from his being seen by a few to his being seen by many," Dwight Sr. says. "Without a doubt, the size of the school doesn't matter. If you can play, they'll see you. But the character of the person does matter."

That character will be tested by fire in the NBA. How will Dwight Howard Jr. handle it?

"God is showing me that I have to stay humble and not let people or fame and other things that go with being the first pick get to me," Junior says. "A lot of people have been selected first, and it's shown in the past that the ones not focused on what they had to do did not succeed in the right way. God has showed me to stay focused on Him and do my job, and not to focus on anything that will stand in the way of worshiping Him."

A Little Help Along the Way

In over 40 years as a sports executive, in major league baseball first and then in the NBA for three decades, Pat Williams has had every type of professional athlete under his guidance. From Julius Erving to Pete Maravich to Moses Malone to Shaq O'Neal, Williams has seen it all. He knows what Howard will face:

• The hangers-on who will talk sweet to Dwight but only want his money and to be found in the reflection of

his fame (read: those who want to be in the proverbial "entourage")
- The women who will want Dwight to forsake his Christian values—just for a little while, they say
- The fans who will love him—only if he delivers

"The temptations are very real," Williams says. "But Dwight seems to be a strong kid, well anchored. I'm impressed with his family. His dad is a real pillar of strength. As Dwight Howard Sr. said when he announced that Dwight's older cousin was coming down to live with him, 'I'll be watching both of them.'"

Dwight Sr. reiterated that promise, but he truly doesn't expect to have to wield a heavy hand. "We will be with him a lot," he says. "Not day-to-day, but a lot, most of the time. I think he'll continue to seek our guidance."

Remember the line from an old song, "Devil with a blue dress on"? He'll see a few of those things. Temptations will linger in every town, in the hotels and restaurants and anywhere else he goes.

"He'll have choices to make," says veteran Magic center Andrew DeClercq, a man of strong Christian faith. "I definitely want to help him. It's exciting to have him on my team, especially with the faith he's publicly professed. In a lot of ways, it's going to be a breath of fresh air to have him here. On the other hand, I hope to offer him a lot of wisdom. I want to be a friend any way I can."

DeClercq believes Dwight's faith in Christ is the key ingredient in enabling an effective transition, because it will drive who he hangs out with and will make the difference in his choices. "The biggest thing is to have support behind you," DeClercq says. "Going into the NBA is a tough transition at any age, on the court and off.

"His faith is something he'll need to keep himself positive and to keep perspective on life. We've got some good veterans to step up and help him, guys who know what he is facing and who come from the Christian perspective, like Grant Hill.

"He's got to keep guys around him who'll be strong. Guys that won't take him to the clubs or places where the girls are. It'll be tough socially, because everywhere he goes he'll be recognized.

There will be women who want to be close to him."

And sharks who want his money. And friends who really aren't. Dwight Jr.'s take on the personal challenges ahead?

"The key is not getting too tempted," he says. "It's good to let loose and hang and have fun, but I have to say to myself, 'This is the wrong situation for me to be in—let me get out of it.'

"I've been in situations like that now—girls trying to do certain stuff. I say, 'I'm not about that, there are bigger goals in life' or 'I'm not about that, I want to be somebody in life.'

"I want to be the greatest basketball player on Earth, and I don't want to talk with anyone who can't help me reach that. There will be a lot of people trying to pull me down, and that motivates me to keep going. God has put me in the greatest situation, and I don't want to take it for granted."

Can He Do It—on the Court and Off?

"If I was ever going to bet on a kid . . ." Pat Williams, who essentially did bet on Dwight Howard Jr. by drafting him, speaks slowly and repeats himself for emphasis. "If I was ever going to bet on a kid, it would be this kid."

"He really has a sense of who is, and whose he is," Williams says. "His walk with Christ seems consistent and very real. But we also have to remember that the evil one never leaves us alone. He is always prowling, and he's very patient, and he's very cagey, very smart. He's not going to win in the long run, but he knows where we're vulnerable. That's why accountability to others is so important."

That's where the faith comes in. Faith in Christ is the cornerstone for Howard, but to the doubter it's the wild card in an otherwise American dream story. The nonbeliever might wonder if it will make him soft or flaky—or both. What difference is his faith really going to make? Does it matter that much? The questions were posed to Williams, he of breadth and depth of experience with so many superstars.

"I think it's his only hope, very frankly," Williams says, his excited, fast-paced speaking tone tempered for a moment. "The pressure is great. There are a lot of side roads players go down, and some go a long way down them, and some go part way and make it back. It's tough enough to play basketball; the side roads complicate things. Those side roads (the wrong women, fame, drugs, misuse of money) can produce a lot of scars. I think being so anchored with his spiritual roots is what gives Dwight Howard the chance to stay on the main highway, stay on a straight line, so that he can focus on professional basketball."

Basketball is Howard's focus. The rest is merely competition for his focus. His greatest athletic goal: to be the best player in basketball. Period. His spiritual goals are related; he has been criticized for his dream of a cross being added to the NBA logo. The media have reminded him that NBA commissioner David Stern is Jewish. So is Jesus.

Howard says he won't be aggressive about sharing his faith, but it's the key part of who he is, so he won't hide it either. He knows the platform of NBA superstardom, should he achieve it, could allow him to impact untold numbers spiritually. Williams says, "He could touch America; he could touch the world. We've never seen it [before] in a player this young."

Williams paused and thought aloud for about a minute, trying to come up with a player so young, with such a strong faith and such talent. David Robinson's faith matured a little later in life. A. C. Green was very good but not a megastar. "We've never seen this combination," Williams decided. "An athlete who becomes the very best in his profession, who keeps his walk clean and unspotted and is unashamed of it. He could touch the world, because basketball and soccer are truly the two world sports.

"Having said that, the most important thing he has to do—I don't want to overspiritualize this—is outwork everybody in this business and take his game to the next level. Let's get that platform first."

That alarm clock is going off. It's early, but it's time.

"I'm the first pick—I've got to be a superstar," Dwight says. "I want to be a superstar. I know it will take a little time to get adjusted to the NBA, but I'm willing to do whatever it takes to be the best. I'm going to succeed the right way. God has shown me [how] to stay focused. I'm not going to let anything get in my way of worshiping Him or being the best basketball player."

PAUL AZINGER

PROFESSIONAL GOLF TOUR VETERAN

In late October 1999, the golf world bade an emotional goodbye to the late Payne Stewart at a memorial service in Orlando, Florida. PGA tour veteran Paul Azinger found himself in the un-enviable role of trying to comfort not only the more than 3,000 mourners in attendance, but also tens of millions who were watching on television around the world.

Remembering his close friend's sense of humor, Azinger rolled up his pants to imitate knickers and wore a tam o'shanter cap, in tribute to the trademark golf attire Stewart wore throughout his career. Then, though tears of grief, Azinger eulogized Payne with a poignant message: "Whoever you are, wherever you are, whatever you have done, if you feel the tug of God's spirit on your heart, do not turn away."

Azinger knows all too well how life can turn on a dime. Azinger was at the top of his game by 1993—averaging one Tour victory every year since 1987—when he was suddenly diagnosed with lymphoma in his right shoulder. A four-time member of the Ryder Cup squad, Azinger played in only four Tour events in 1994 while undergoing cancer treatment. He returned the following year and was given the Golf Writers Association of America's Ben Hogan Award, and wrote *Zinger*, a book about his victory over cancer. His last tour victory occurred at the 2000 Sony Open in Hawaii; and he ultimately racked up an impressive career record of 12 PGA Tour wins through 2004.

Although he continues to play a partial Tour schedule, in 2005, Azinger joined *ABC Sports* as an analyst for PGA events. Those who subscribe to Sky Angel network got a glimpse of Azinger when he appeared with other Christian athletes for an alternative halftime show during Super Bowl XXXIX. More recently, Azinger has taken an active role in the Ryder Cup, assuming the duties of captain for the 2008 U.S. team.

Azinger resides in Florida with his wife, Toni, and two daughters.

CHANGING COURSE

By Terry Tush

Paul Azinger's drive to golf's pinnacle was halted by an obstacle he now calls "one of the greatest experiences of my life."

Paul Azinger was almost at the top. He had moved tantalizingly close to the highest echelon of golf's elite players.

Always before, it seemed, his career had been like the 40-foot putt that stopped on the lip of the cup and never fell in.

The former Florida State University standout had joined the PGA Tour in 1982 and had steadily made his ascent on the money list. He became the tour's second-leading money winner in 1987, was third in 1989 and fourth in 1990.

Yet there had been so many disappointments. There was the 1987 British Open when he bogeyed the last hole to lose to Nick Faldo. He had lost about a half dozen other major tournaments on the final nine holes of play. And, of course, he kept being reminded that he had never won one of the four majors.

But 1993 was different.

Azinger won his first major title, the PGA Championship at Inverness, by defeating Greg Norman in a two-hole playoff. He finished second on the PGA Tour money list, earning more than $1.4 million. Azinger also won two other tournaments that year, bringing his career total at that time to 11. His 10 top-3 finishes were the most on the tour since Tom Watson's in 1980. He kept his 7-year-long tournament victory streak alive, giving him the longest such run on the Tour. In addition, he played a key role in the U.S. victory in the Ryder Cup that year.

Finally, Paul Azinger had climbed his way to the peak of success. It was the type of year every professional golfer dreams about.

Until December. That final month of 1993, a month usually full of celebration and family, turned ugly for Azinger. Doctors discovered that he had lymphoma—a form of cancer—in his right shoulder blade.

"I had a jolt through my system," recalls Azinger. "You don't expect anyone to tell you when you're 33 years old that you've got cancer."

His thoughts turned immediately to his wife, Toni, and daughters, Sarah Jean and Josie Lynn.

Although Dr. Frank Jobe, the PGA Tour medical director, told him that 90 percent of all lymphoma patients recover completely, Azinger didn't feel so fortunate.

But he wasn't left without hope.

"When something like this happens, you can scream, 'Why me? Why me, God?' You can run away or you can do an about-face and run to God, and cling to Him for your hope," Azinger says.

"That's what I did. I just ran to God. I realized I was not in control of my life. God allows things to happen [for reasons] we don't always know or understand. But I came to realize that if this is His call for me, I'm willing to accept it.

"I think my greatest hope is in the truth of the Bible—and that's eternal life through Jesus Christ. That's where my security lies. That's where my hope lies."

Within minutes of being informed he had cancer, Azinger went to a nearby hospital where he underwent a CAT scan and bone marrow tests. Dr. Jobe wanted to make sure the cancer had not spread.

Then Azinger took his family back to a hotel, where they waited for three days to get the test results. "Those three days of not knowing were a life-changing experience for me in a lot of ways," he says.

"It was a time to collect my thoughts, to ask myself a lot of things.

"I thought about mortality for the first time. I could be covered with cancer. I could die from it. Cancer knows no age. I looked on life from an eternal perspective."

When the results finally returned, they revealed that the lymphoma had not spread. Nonetheless, Azinger immediately began monthly chemotherapy treatments, which would continue until May 1994.

"Mentally, I was prepared to not get sick," Azinger says. "I can honestly say that I did not know what sick was until I did my first one [chemotherapy treatment]."

He awoke about 11 o'clock the night of his first chemotherapy treatment. "I just lay in bed for an hour knowing I was going to get sick," Azinger said. The chemicals were taking their toll on his body. He started vomiting and did so every 20 minutes for 9 hours.

Three weeks later, Azinger awoke one morning to find clumps of his hair on the pillow. It also happened to be the day the Azingers hosted Sarah Jean's eighth birthday party. As the party came to a close, and the 10 screaming girls went out to the front yard, Azinger decided to make it a party none of them would ever forget. The girls lined up and began pulling his hair out in clumps.

"It didn't hurt a bit," he says. "It was a denial for me that ended up turning into something fun. Besides, bald is in—look at all the basketball players shaving their heads."

Azinger made his first public appearance May 16 in Tulsa, Oklahoma, the site of the 1994 PGA Championship, and he declared himself cancer-free.

"Those six months [during the chemotherapy treatment] went pretty fast, and I thank God for that," recalls Azinger. "I was guilty, even as a Christian, of trying to get my happiness from where I was on the money list or from winning championships. There's nothing anyone can accomplish in this world that can bring the happiness I'm feeling right now.

"I know that when you're 33, you're not bullet-proof. I'm as vulnerable as the next guy. None of us is promised tomorrow. We need to live every day to the fullest."

Azinger was surprised by the attention he received during his six-month battle with lymphoma. "I had planned on answering all of the letters . . ." But when the total reached nearly 15,000, he reconsidered.

Some days, he received more than 40 telephone calls. Among those who called were former President George H. Bush, now-retired Georgia Senator Sam Nunn, Florida State football coach Bobby Bowden, then-New England Patriots football coach Bill Parcells and just about every player on the PGA Tour.

One of the calls that Azinger will always remember came from Johnny Miller. "He told me, 'Zinger, it's not always what we accomplish in life that matters, it's what we overcome. You have to overcome something far greater than what most people have to overcome. That's the reality you're facing.' And he's right."

Soon after learning of his cancer, Azinger made it a goal to defend his PGA Championship title at Southern Hills Country Club in Tulsa. He did play in the tourney, but unfortunately, didn't make the cut and, thus, couldn't defend his title. Yet he was able to put everything into perspective.

"If doctors told me, 'Zinger, you can't play golf anymore,' I would be all right," he says. "This whole ordeal, this has been one of the greatest experiences of my life. I can honestly say that. One of the best things about it is that it's given me a forum to encourage and inspire a lot of people. It's taught me a lot."

Paul Azinger worked hard to get to the top of the golfing world, but it was his illness that taught him what it truly means to be a champion.

JASON SCHMIDT

PITCHING ACE

Like so many young boys with baseball dreams, eight-year-old Jason
Schmidt looked out over the field . . .
and saw his future. On that summer
day in 1981, while attending a Seattle
Mariners game, he announced to his
father that one day he was going to
be a major league pitcher.

But unlike so many boys his age,
little Jason's prediction came true—in
a very big way.

Jason Schmidt made his major league pitching debut with
Atlanta in 1995. After a brief stop in Pittsburgh, Schmidt was traded to San Francisco in 2001, where he quickly blossomed into one
of baseball's most dominant pitchers of the new millennium.

Blessed with a smoking fastball and one of the game's best
changeups, the 6' 5" right-hander was arguably the most feared
starter in the National League during the 2003 and 2004 seasons.
In 2003, after going 17-5 and striking out 208 in 207.2 innings,
Schmidt finished second in the voting for the NL Cy Young Award,
and his off-the-field benevolence earned him the Giants Roberto
Clemente Award.

The following year, he did even better, posting an 18-7 record,
a 3.20 earned run average and striking out a whopping 251 batters
in just 225 innings—a single-season record for all Giant pitchers.
For his efforts that year, Schmidt was named the Players' Choice
NL Outstanding Pitcher of the Year, as well as the *Sporting News* NL
Pitcher of the Year.

Injury was the only opponent that could even attempt to challenge Schmidt's dominance, as he made a handful of trips to the dis-
abled list, eventually going under the knife for shoulder and elbow
surgery. But in June 2006 he roared back, striking out 16 Florida

Marlins hitters and tying a team record for most strikeouts in a single game. In 2007, Schmidt inked a massive three-year, $47 million dollar contract to pitch for San Francisco's NL West Division rival, the Los Angeles Dodgers.

Yet for all that, Jason Schmidt's real priorities haven't changed much from his early years in the minor leagues. He's still a committed believer. He still wants more from life than time on the mound. Sure, he loves what he does at the ballpark, but he wants to be remembered for who is—a follower of Christ—not just what he does. If the past is any indication of what his future holds, Schmidt is off to a great start.

FEELING IT

By Mark Moran

The death of Jason Schmidt's mom has had a profound effect on the pitcher, his game and his life.

The 2003 season turned out to be a career year for Jason Schmidt of the San Francisco Giants. The lanky right-hander picked up a career-high 17 victories, and he led the National League with a 2.34 ERA.

So he must have been terribly worried that his off-season elbow surgery was going to hinder his chances at another run for the Cy Young Award. He must have brooded about whether that 40-minute operation to repair a torn elbow ligament would hold together during pitching outings. *Would he still be able to be among the league-leaders in sacrifice bunts? Would he still touch the upper 90s on the radar gun with his fastball? Would he make some of the National League's scariest hitters wilt in the batter's box?*

These questions surely must have kept Jason Schmidt up at night. Right?

Not even close. While Schmidt does certainly give those things a lot of thought and he has a drive to win baseball games, the burning question on the top of Jason Schmidt's mind has nothing to do with anything that happens between the white lines on a baseball field. He's concerned with much deeper issues. "Do enough people really know what I stand for and what I believe in?" Schmidt wonders aloud.

Schmidt's mother, Vicki, died of a brain tumor in April 2003. The hundreds of people who gathered for her funeral sounded a common theme: She was a person who was devoted to her family and to Christ. As he sat there listening, Schmidt was flooded with emotions, and he began to reflect on what matters most in life.

"People are always going to remember me for baseball," he says. "Is that really the real reason we're here? I would like to be remembered as a Christian athlete. When we pass away, what are people going to say? Are they going to know what you stood for? They're gonna know when I pass away where I'm going. That's the No. 1 thing."

Vicki's death proved difficult for Schmidt, his family and his friends. "That was a hard phone call to make," says veteran pitcher and Schmidt's friend Russ Ortiz, who phoned Schmidt just after Vicki's death. "He's such a good friend that I couldn't help but start crying."

If there is any silver lining in this dark cloud, Ortiz says he thinks Schmidt's mother's death actually made Jason a stronger Christian. "When your perspective and your priority is Jesus, whatever happens, you know you can still get through it. And it seems to me right now, that's where he's at," Ortiz says of Schmidt. "He's become a better person and a better player because of everything he's gone through."

Jason Schmidt grew up in a Christian home in Washington State, and he knew well the ins and outs of church life. His father was a pastor. "I think I set an attendance record for Sunday School. I was there Sunday morning, Sunday night, Wednesday night. Whatever they had, I was always there," Schmidt says.

He excelled in baseball and basketball at Kelso High School in southwest Washington, and even though he knew he was going to be drafted as a pitcher, he played football his senior year.

Just after graduation, the Atlanta Braves came calling—the circumstances of which tested Schmidt. "It was my first time away from home. I was 18 years old," he says. "I thought I would try it my way for a while. I didn't have to go church on Sunday. I didn't have a curfew. I thought, *Hey, I can do whatever I want.* So I went out and tested the waters for a few years," Schmidt says. "But I did some things I wasn't real proud of, and I started to miss my Christian friends and going to church."

Schmidt originally signed to play baseball with the University of Arizona Wildcats in Tucson, prompted by the image in his mind of what he thought big league players looked like. "I thought every guy was 6' 5", 250 pounds and hitting 550-foot home runs. I thought, *Here I am 6' 5", 185 pounds—I'm going to get killed out there.* So I'm going to go to college and put on another 20 to 30 pounds before I'm ready. But then they start waving the contract in your face, and the next thing you know, I was out there."

Literally. Schmidt was spirited off to Bradenton, Florida, far from his home in Kelso, where he had been the state player of the year and an All-State MVP in 1991. Where he had thrown a no-hitter, striking out 20 of the 21 batters he faced. Where it had all seemed to come so easily.

Bradenton was definitely not Kelso. "Nobody there," Schmidt recalls. "It was typical rookie ball. Guys told me that if you pitch well you can get outta here and go to Single A ball. My motivation was to pitch well enough to get out of there," he says, laughing.

Schmidt did move up the following year. Then it was on to Double A in 1994. In 1995, he broke training camp on the Braves roster.

Schmidt honed more than his pitching skills in the minors. He was and still is known and feared in many a major league clubhouse for another reason. "He's a practical joker," says Earl Smith. Smith was chapel leader for the San Francisco Giants, the team Schmidt had been pitching with since 2001. Smith has watched

Schmidt grow as a ballplayer and a person over the last few years, and while he's wary of Schmidt's penchant for practical jokes, he likes to watch the master at work.

That's because Smith suspects Schmidt the jokester is actually up to something else. "He's loose in the clubhouse and he uses his humor to let his faith show through," Smith says.

Ortiz, who was on the Giants pitching staff with Schmidt in 2001 and 2002, isn't always quick with a laugh when it comes to Schmidt's whimsy. "You never feel completely comfortable when he's around," he says. "It's like he's always got some scheme up his sleeve."

According to some clubhouse accounts, Schmidt has developed quite a repertoire of antics, melding his top-drawer material with some of the stuff he's picked up along the way. The most reliable of Schmidt's tricks? "Probably the gum that shocks you when you try to take it out of the pack," Ortiz says. "He keeps it pretty tame, but sometimes he gets in a streak where he does a lot. You're always on the lookout when he's around."

While Schmidt's teammates have spent a lot of time looking over their shoulder in the clubhouse, it was Schmidt's shoulder that his Pittsburgh Pirates were really concerned about in 2000. That's when Schmidt missed most of the season with problems in his pitching shoulder. Finally, on August 8 that year, he underwent season-ending arthroscopic surgery on his right shoulder. The damage was so severe Schmidt thought his career might be over.

Ironically, the injury turned his life around. "I was at my wits' end," he says. "I didn't know if I was going to pitch again. I would go home at night and I just felt lonely. I could be in the clubhouse and I'd feel lonely. I just had that empty feeling that everybody talks about, and I knew what it was. I opened up my Bible and started reading during spring training, and everything just made sense. The Bible had never made sense to me like that before. All of a sudden, everything clicked. Just like pitching. I couldn't put it down. I could not wait for practice to get over so that I could get home and lie in my bed and read the Bible. It changed my life. It was a supernatural thing."

After overcoming the shoulder injury, Schmidt pitched half of the 2001 season for the Pirates until he was traded to San Francisco on July 30 that year.

The next year, he won 13 games for the Giants and led them to the World Series against the Anaheim Angels. He was the only member of the Giants starting rotation to post a victory in the Fall Classic. The Giants fell to the Angels in seven games after being just a few outs away from winning it in San Francisco. "That one was the most disappointing because we were so close," Schmidt says.

Schmidt did his part to get the Giants back to the Series in 2003, posting 17 victories, fashioning the National League's best ERA, holding his opponents to the league's lowest batting average and earning his way onto the All-Star team for the first time. He also finished second in balloting for the National League Cy Young Award. The Giants were beaten in the first round of the playoffs by the eventual World Series champion Florida Marlins.

Despite some heartbreaking playoff losses, Schmidt has become one of the dominant pitchers in the game, largely, he says, because of a dramatic change in his attitude that came after rededicating his life to Christ. "I no longer felt the need to go out and perform at a level I wasn't capable of," he says.

Ortiz has noticed a change in his friend. "He has more of a peace about him," Ortiz says. But don't mistake that spiritual peace for a lack of ferocity on the mound. Schmidt wants to win as badly as the next guy. He's had some pretty impressive teachers early in his career. Imagine breaking into the bigs under the instruction of Tom Glavine, Greg Maddux and John Smoltz.

"I had so much stuff coming in, I didn't know how to filter it all," Schmidt says. "There would be times when I would come in from a game and Smoltz would say I threw too many sliders, Maddux would say I threw too many fastballs, and then Glavine would say I threw too many curveballs. Every game I had a different Cy Young guy coming up and telling me what I did wrong," Schmidt remembers with a chuckle.

"I didn't know what to do. If I had listened to all of them, I wouldn't have thrown anything up there." Some of the things those masters of the mound told Schmidt that didn't make sense then are crystal-clear now. But the one piece of advice that drives Schmidt perhaps more than any other was given to him in 2001 by veteran Terry Mulholland when the two were with the Pirates.

"You've got 4 or 5 pitches when you're on the mound, and you're in control," Mulholland told him. "They don't know if you're gonna throw a 90-mile-per-hour fastball or a 95-mile-per-hour fastball. They don't know if it's gonna be high or low. The ball is in your court. You can do anything you want to and that's the fun of the game." Schmidt credits that advice and his work ethic, which includes plenty of bookwork, for his dominating performances the last few seasons.

Taking a page from Red Sox ace Curt Schilling, Schmidt diligently studies the hitters he will face prior to each game, poring over reams of computer-generated stats. "Hitters are studying you, so you better study them," Schmidt says. "Anybody can hit a 95-mile-per-hour fastball if they know it's comin'," he says. "You gotta be able to put the ball where you want it. And more than that, you gotta know when to put it where you want it. It wasn't until I really started studying hitters and studying the game and studying the art of pitching and the mechanics that things kind of clicked for me," he says.

Russ Ortiz says that preparation has been one of the keys to Schmidt's success, particularly in recent years. "Watching how he prepares for a game and stays focused once he's pitching is pretty impressive," Ortiz says. "I think the consistency that I've seen in him is why he's done so well. I used to ask him if he would ever take a day off once in a while."

While Ortiz and Schmidt don't always agree on the best way to approach every hitter, Ortiz says the two were good for each other when they were both with the Giants. "We were always willing to listen and learn from each other and better our relationship on and off the field. That's what a friendship is all about," Ortiz says. Now that the two are with different teams, though, the bonds of that friendship can be stretched only so far. "I always told him if he ever faced me, he would never get a hit," Ortiz says. "I always gave him grief about how bad his swing is."

Jokes, practical and otherwise, aside, Jason Schmidt may not have all the answers to life's most important issues. But at least he's asking the right questions, including one that drives his life: "What kind of impact do we have on other people's lives?"

LADAINIAN TOMLINSON

NFL MOST VALUABLE PLAYER

LaDainian Tomlinson grew up in north Texas and became a Dallas Cowboys fan, just like his father. Young LaDainian fell in love with football, so when he was 13, his mother sent him to Emmitt Smith's Football Camp.

Little did he know that one day he would be taking handoff after handoff from NFL quarterbacks and chasing Smith's all-time rushing record.

As a matter of fact, if Tomlinson continues to pile up yardage like he has in each of his first six NFL seasons—he's averaged 1,529 yards per year—L. T. will break Smith's record of 18,355 career yards sometime during the 2012 season.

Consistently ranked among the league's top rushers every season he's been a pro, Tomlinson is the game's best all-purpose back. He's averaged 66 receptions and 483 yards each year from 2001 through 2006, and he led the AFC in receptions with 100 in 2003.

Tomlinson already is the Chargers all-time leading rusher and scorer; now his name is becoming commonplace in NFL record books. On November 26, 2006, Tomlinson shattered the great Jim Brown's record for most touchdowns scored in a five-game span by taking it to the house 16 times. But L. T. was just getting warmed up.

On December 10, he recorded his twenty-ninth touchdown of the year, breaking Shawn Alexander's record of 28 set in 2005. (L. T. went on to score 31 total touchdowns in 2006.) The following week, he eclipsed two records while scoring two touchdowns versus the Kansas City Chiefs and capped the season by winning his first NFL rushing title. And his phenomenal year did not go unnoticed nationally. Tomlinson easily won the NFL's Most Valuable Player Award, was named the *Sporting News* 2006 Sportsman of the Year and finished a close second to Tiger Woods in the voting for the Associated Press 2006 Male Athlete of the Year.

In case you think, though, that his only accomplishments are out on the football field, think again. L. T. is a man of faith, who lives in the Word of God and seeks His will, on the field and off. Even amid tragedy, his trust in the Lord is steadfast—he knows that God has a game plan, one that can't be improved upon.

Tomlinson is also a man of action when it comes to helping others. He participates in various charitable causes and heads up the San Diego-based Tomlinson Touching Lives Foundation, which hosts events throughout the year in an effort to assist children and needy families.

POSITIVE YARDAGE

By Kevin Acee

Despite a deep family tragedy, LaDainian Tomlinson keeps moving forward through his faith and for his family.

In a locker room muted by the deflation that comes with a season ended prematurely, LaDainian Tomlinson sat on a stool, head down, his face streaked with the salt of perspiration and tears.

He was, as he does every defeat, absorbing as personal the San Diego Chargers' 20-17 overtime loss to the New York Jets in January 2005.

Through a three-deep throng of reporters that encircled Tomlinson, team chaplain Shawn Mitchell politely moved and bent down until he was near the star running back's ear.

"Remember, you're going to be a daddy," Mitchell said. Up came Tomlinson's head. On it, a smile Mitchell recalls as nothing short of "radiant."

That perspective had carried Tomlinson through the previous months, ever since the summer of 2004 when he found out his wife, LaTorsha, was pregnant with their first child. He was always updating friends with news about LaTorsha's doctor visits and sharing sonogram images of Mckiah Renee, their daughter.

At the beginning of February 2005, Tomlinson went to the Pro Bowl, his second in four seasons in the NFL. Friends and family saw a man fairly floating, elated by the anticipation of his impending fatherhood and the good times that defined his life.

"He was so ready to be a father," Mitchell said.

And then, on February 22, LaDainian and LaTorsha found out their baby daughter had died in the womb. LaTorsha would deliver the baby, but Mckiah Renee would not spend a moment in this world.

And herein lies the story of a man who accepted tragedy the way he has accepted blessings, who turned his focus to heaven when he lost his daughter the same way he did when he signed the most lucrative contract ever awarded an NFL running back.

"I always feel the Lord has a plan for my life," Tomlinson says.

It really does seem that straightforward for the man who might be the world's best at what he does. Time and again, LaDainian Tomlinson does not waiver from his absolute confidence in God's sovereignty.

The seeds of faith are planted by God but cultivated by a man in his own heart. As Tomlinson's friend and former teammate Scott Turner said of Tomlinson's perspective, "That is developed by a life of faith; it doesn't just happen when trials happen."

Ask LaDainian Tomlinson about his relationship with God and he begins by giving credit to his mother and his Texas roots.

"I was raised in the church and everything," he says simply. "I started it at a very young age—going to church and being in the Word and things like that. Especially being from Texas; it's established in you."

But delve deeper and he speaks of a time in high school, "when I started to dominate the competition, I was cocky at times. I didn't like the way I was," that he began to seek out this God of his mother and make Jesus his own. "I felt like I needed my own personal relationship, so I didn't have to rely on what my mom said all the time," he recalls.

That relationship guided him to college at Texas Christian University. He acknowledges the desire he had to play for bigger schools, but those schools did not want him. With time as a teacher, he was able to see the Lord's hand pushing him to TCU.

"He knew I'd meet my wife there," he says, actually giggling.

In her husband, LaTorsha sees an example, a man who prays first thing every morning, on his knees, and motivates her to read the Bible every day. Yet Tomlinson would loathe any suggestion he is special in any way for his reliance on God. He is a man, after all, who keeps no memorabilia from his own growing anthology of highlight moments.

Though he is known around the country simply by his initials, and though his stop-and-go moves routinely have opposing linebackers check for missing drawers, and though he is the highest-paid player in Chargers history, and though he has a jersey that is among the most frequently bought among fans league-wide—he is not impressed. The trappings mean little to LaDainian Tomlinson.

But having millions of dollars and the adoration of thousands does come with its challenges. There is a tendency among us all—and particularly those blessed with skills the world values—to forget who bestowed our talents, to look inward rather than upward. Face it: There are some football-mad people who would not blame Tomlinson if he read Matthew 14 (Jesus walking on water) and thought, *Hey. I could do that.*

Mitchell, the senior pastor at New Life Christian Fellowship in Oceanside, California, and a longtime Chargers chaplain, has seen plenty of that kind of attitude. "A lot of players exude a sense of self-importance," Mitchell says. "On the opposite end of the spectrum you have LaDainian. He portrays an extremely strong image of Jesus Christ."

Mitchell mentions the praying hands tattoo on one of Tomlinson's biceps and his perfect attendance at the team's chapel service, as well as his extensive knowledge of the Bible. More than that,

however, is what Mitchell hears people say about Tomlinson—
coaches, teammates and others who have met Tomlinson have
experienced his humility and charming sense of his place in
the world.

Chargers coach Marty Schottenheimer has on more than
one occasion called Tomlinson the most unique person he has
ever met.

What likely impresses Schottenheimer, a coach in the NFL
since 1984, is that in the strata he and Tomlinson occupy, the consistency with which Tomlinson is above reproach is extremely rare.

"What I've noticed about him is through all the success he's
had, all the financial blessings, the guy has never changed," says
former teammate DeQuincy Scott. "Sometimes when people get a
few more dollars—especially when they haven't had money before—
they think they're on top of the world. L. T. just takes it as a blessing from God and acts that way."

Professional athletes face the same challenges to their faith as
do those with not quite so many zeroes behind their bank balance. And they face different ones. Relatives and friends asking
for money, the risk of pride, the ready availability of every manner
of vice that comes with fame and fortune. "It's tough because of
outside things—the temptations the devil is always trying to bring
on you through different people trying to get what you have,"
Tomlinson acknowledges.

Says LaTorsha, "Being in the NFL, it comes along with a lot of
other things that aren't so good. It's great just watching him deal
with it and having that confidence in him and watching him
always turn to God when he's confused about something."

With a laugh that is a little sad because of what her comment
means about men without Jesus as their foundation, LaTorsha
says, "It's extremely difficult to be the wife of an NFL player. I don't
think we get enough credit, honestly. When your husband is close
to the Lord and in the Word every day, it makes it so much easier."

It makes more bearable the every day and the bad days.

Because of who he is and has long been—the young man who
spoke almost exclusively about his mother on their first date

and who took her to church a short while after that—LaTorsha Tomlinson's husband helped her through a time she thought she might not survive. She emerged with her faith not only intact but also stronger.

"God definitely used LaDainian for me," LaTorsha says of the loss of their child. "I was a wreck. There are days still when I'm a wreck. LaDainian is my rock. He sacrificed his own need to grieve, pushed it to the back, to stand up and be there for me. I know that was God telling him, 'She's going to need you.' I'll be honest: I was angry. It took LaDainian to tell me, 'God has a plan.' "

LaDainian has said he thought the key moment in his wife's recovery came during a difficult day when she went to lie outside by the couple's pool. A butterfly landed on her toe.

"We took that as a sign," LaDainian Tomlinson says. "It was like God was telling us our daughter was okay."

LaTorsha Tomlinson remembers a different watershed moment. She was lying in bed, unable to get out because of her sadness. LaDainian came and sat by her, and among the things he said was a reminder that they don't know the big picture, but God does.

"I'll never forget that," LaTorsha says. "I cried and cried. But I knew he was right."

All this stoutness and dependence on God does not mean LaDainian Tomlinson has not grieved his daughter. "I'd be driving down the street and think about her and start crying," he says. "Still to this day there are good days and bad days."

But, still, there is this: "I understood God's plan. I never really questioned God. I just felt like He knows everything. He knows the number of hairs on my head, so why would I ever question Him?"

MARY LOU RETTON

GOLD MEDAL WINNING GYMNAST

The gold medal. The Wheaties boxes. That all-American smile. It's hard to believe that more than 20 years have passed since Mary Lou Retton vaulted herself to international fame by winning five medals at the 1984 Summer Olympics—including the first gold medal in gymnastics ever won by an American woman. Today, she remains one of this country's most recognized and admired sports personalities.

The all-American girl has become the all-American mom. Mary Lou and her husband, former Texas Longhorn quarterback Shannon Kelley, are the proud parents of four children. Her and her husband's love of children has led to a PBS television series titled, "Mary Lou's Flip Flop Shop," which she and Shannon created. The programs help teach life lessons to children between the ages of four and seven, and encourages them to lead healthy lifestyles.

Over the years, Retton has served as a color commentator on network Olympic broadcasts, made appearances in movies and on television series, and has been a guest on the Christian Broadcasting Network (CBN), as well as other Christian programs. She also has served as the national chairperson for the Children's Miracle Network.

Retton is the author of two books: *Mary Lou: Creating an Olympic Champion* and *Mary Lou Retton's Gateway to Happiness: Seven Ways to a More Peaceful, More Prosperous, More Satisfying Life*. As a highly sought-after motivational speaker, Retton speaks at churches and to mainstream audiences around the country and is active with the Washington Speaker's Bureau.

She is also a member of the USOC Olympic Hall of Fame, the International Gymnastics Hall of Fame and the Texas Sports Hall of Fame.

A NEW ROUTINE

By Christin Ditchfield

Famous for her remarkable gymnastics performances, Mary Lou Retton is comfortable in a totally different role.

It was one of the greatest moments in Olympic history.

For 9 years of her young life, Mary Lou Retton had worked toward this moment. She needed a 9.95 to earn a tie for the individual All-Around gymnastics title at the 1984 Olympics in Los Angeles. She needed perfection to win the title outright.

As half the world sat riveted to their television sets, the diminutive 16-year-old gymnast hurtled down the runway toward the vaulting horse. Hitting the springboard, she flipped through the air and nailed a perfect landing.

The 9,000 spectators in the Pauley Pavilion leaped to their feet, screaming wildly. In homes around the globe, people smiled, cheered and cried tears of joy for the teenager from West Virginia.

Retton had just vaulted her way to Olympic superstardom, earning a perfect 10. The flawless vault propelled Retton ahead of Romania's Ecaterina Szabo and onto the podium as the youngest U.S. gymnast ever to win a medal and the first American woman to capture gold in any gymnastic event. Later in the week she added two silvers and two bronzes to her collection. Retton's total of five medals topped that of any other athlete in the 1984 Summer Games.

Suddenly, Mary Lou was an international celebrity. Her exuberant smile brightened the covers of *Life* magazine, *Seventeen*, *Sports Illustrated*, *Time* and *Newsweek*. She did dozens of TV interviews and talk shows. Retton had the honor of being the first female athlete to be pictured on a Wheaties cereal box. She received numerous awards and accolades. Fan letters poured in from all over the globe.

For some athletes, Olympic glory fades quickly. They pick up their medals, enjoy the glare of the spotlight for weeks, maybe months. But then the crowds go away, reporters stop calling, and they wander back into anonymity.

For Mary Lou Retton, the spotlight has never faded.

Many years after her Olympic triumph, Mary Lou is still one of the most popular and widely recognized athletes in the world. While her athletic accomplishments are impressive, they alone cannot account for her phenomenal popularity. After all, there have been many other athletes whose achievements have been just as significant.

There were other Americans at the 1984 Games who earned gold medals. Somehow, what Mary Lou accomplished and how she did it reached out and touched the hearts of millions. And nothing has happened in the intervening years to weaken that bond.

Mary Lou Retton was born and raised in Fairmont, a tiny coal-mining town in West Virginia. She was the youngest of five children in a close, happy Italian-American family. Retton was the quintessential girl-next-door, reminding everyone of their daughter or sister or niece. She was bubbly and friendly and down-to-earth, radiating confidence and charm.

But it was Retton's powerful and dynamic style that rocked the gymnastics world. In many ways, 16-year-old Mary Lou embodied the American dream back in 1984. From humble beginnings, she had risen to the pinnacle of her sport, achieving her goals through extraordinary determination and hard work. And she did it with heart-warming enthusiasm.

Although she retired from competition in 1986, Mary Lou has remained active in the athletic community. For example, she has worked as a TV commentator for NBC. In the 1992 and 1996 Games, she wrote a regular column for *USA Today* and hosted an Olympic Highlights television show. She has also served as an advisor to the President's Council on Physical Fitness.

In addition to her ongoing work in sports, Mary Lou has devoted much of her time to charities. She occasionally guest stars on TV shows and in movies.

Mary Lou is happily married and living in Houston, Texas, with her husband Shannon Kelley, and their four girls: Shayla, McKenna, Skyla and Emma. Mary Lou's fame and her personality have made her a popular conference speaker and a sought-after spokesperson for a wide variety of corporations, organizations and causes. For a number of years, she's been on the speaker's circuit, talking about winning and her Olympic experiences.

But recently, she's found herself speaking out about something much more personal. "I'm a Christian," Retton says. "I believe in Jesus Christ, who died on the cross for my sins."

When people hear about Retton's faith, they assume it must be a recent experience. Not so.

"I grew up in a very Christian home," she says. "I've had the Lord in my heart [since I was young]. But since my husband and I got married, I've grown so much closer to God. We belong to a young couples' Bible study group—it's great fellowship! I love our church and our pastor."

While faith in Christ is not new for her, talking about it publicly is. Mary Lou admits that she hasn't discussed her faith in public very often, largely because of her personality and her public image.

"I've never been an in-your-face type of person," she explains. "I've always been 'sweet Mary Lou.' For years I felt that I needed to please everybody, make everybody happy, make everybody smile. They tell you not to talk about things like politics and religion because it's something everyone's going to disagree on—you know, 'Don't rock the boat!' The most important thing to me was being a Christian deep inside, knowing Jesus was in my heart."

For years, Mary Lou has been content to witness about her Christian faith through her lifestyle. So why speak up now? The answer is found in the maturity that comes with motherhood.

"I guess I'm at a different stage in my life," Retton says. "I'm a wife, I'm a mother. I've realized that I need to set that example in a more vocal way, in a public way, for my daughters. And part of being a Christian is getting the word out."

That growing sense of responsibility has led Mary Lou to look for opportunities to talk about her faith with others. She began mentioning her faith in interviews and on talk-show appearances. And she appeared in a series of television spots produced by the Southern Baptist Convention in its "Celebrate Jesus 2000" evangelistic campaign.

As if she needed something else to do.

These days, the biggest challenge for "Mary Lou the Mom" is finding time for all the things on her schedule. She's juggling speaking engagements, volunteer work and commercial shoots with her responsibilities as a wife and homemaker. Add to that the new requests from organizations who are asking her to talk about her faith.

"It's really, really hard," she admits. "It takes a lot of organization and a lot of preparation on a daily basis. I'm on the road giving motivational speeches to different companies and making appearances. But my family is my first priority. My No. 1 job is to be a wife and mother. So when it comes to my schedule, I have to set limits. I try not to work on weekends because weekends are family time. I don't leave home for more than one night at a time. When I am home, I'm there 24 hours a day."

Retton acknowledges that a schedule like hers could take its toll on any marriage, so she and Shannon work hard to keep their relationship going strong.

"I'm so blessed that the Lord brought Shannon and me together," she says. "We dated for five or six years before we got married. We literally grew up together. My husband is truly my best friend—and my No. 1 fan. I'm just so blessed."

A go-getter like Mary Lou always has something new to consider—new goals, projects, dreams. She's accustomed to pursuing those things with the same determination and drive that propelled her to the height of Olympic glory.

Lately, though, Mary Lou says she's been learning about patience. "There are things I've been working on for years, asking

God for His guidance and direction. But it doesn't work on my timeline; it works on the Lord's timeline. That's been very frustrating to me! The society we live in says, 'I want it, and I want it now!' I'm trying to accept that sometimes my prayers are answered 'No.' Sometimes when the Lord doesn't give me something or answer my prayer right away, He's protecting me. I may not be ready for a certain thing at this point in my life. I just have to be patient and totally trust Him."

Retton has a piece of paper taped to her desk that reads: "Good morning! This is God. I will be handling all of your problems today. I will not need your help. So have a good day!"

"Isn't that great!" exclaims Retton. "I love it! That's what I try to live my day by, not stressing over the little things, the things that are out of our control. 'Cause we can worry ourselves sick—and worry is such a sin! Just give it to God!"

Another perfect 10 from Mary Lou.

CHRISTIAN HOSOI

EXTREME SKATEBOARDER

Just as the high-flying aerobatics of Michael Jordan revolutionized the game of basketball, so did the gravity-defying moves of Christian Hosoi transform skateboarding from a schoolyard hobby into a financially lucrative business and internationally recognized sport. Throughout the 1980s, Hosoi attained legendary status for inventing jaw-dropping aerial moves, at one point holding the world record.

Although Michael Jordan is retired from basketball, he remains involved in the NBA as managing member of operations for the Charlotte Bobcats. Similarly, Hosoi remains visible and highly active in the sport he helped put on the map. After his 2004 release from prison (where he'd served five years on a drug conviction), Hosoi charged back into the world of skateboarding. He hooked up as a team rider with mega-sponsor Quiksilver, joining such stars as Arto Saari, Omar Hassan, Bastien Salabanzi and longtime friend and skateboarding legend Tony Hawk.

A cutting-edge skateboard developer himself, Hosoi formed Hosoi Skates back in the 1980s and created what became skateboarding's most popular board, the Hammerhead. Just as Michael Jordan leapt over Madison Avenue with his Air Jordans in the '80s, in 2006 Hosoi had a pro-model skateboarding shoe named after him—the Hosoi Sk8-Hi 4.

Hosoi is featured on Tony Hawk's *Project 8* video game; and in November 2006, Hosoi's life became the subject of a 99-minute documentary film titled *Rising Son: The Legend of Skateboarder Christian*

Hosoi. Narrated by actor Dennis Hopper, the film documents Hosoi's beginnings as a skateboarder in the West Los Angeles suburbs where he grew up, to his rise to the top of the skateboarding world and the turbulent lifestyle that accompanied it—including his incarceration, his release from prison and his newfound Christian faith. The film features cameo appearances by Tony Hawk and other professional skateboarders, as well as interviews with friends and members of Hosoi's family.

While Hosoi will tell you that his wife, Jennifer, and son, Christian Classic Kamea, are two of the most important people in his life, he'll then share with you that another is Jesus Christ. After his encounter with the Lord in prison, Hosoi experienced a complete conversion—the kind that only grace can bring about and only grace can sustain. Today, this skateboarding legend continues to spread the good news and help others find true freedom in Christ.

FRESH AIR
By Micah McDaniel

Not many superstar athletes end up in prison; even fewer are as dedicated as Christian Hosoi to sharing the gospel message.

Smack! Never before has the sound of a judge's gavel pounding down a sentence been music to a convicted felon's ears, but to Christian Hosoi the tune couldn't have been sweeter.

For the skateboarding legend, his 70-month sentence was a gift. After being arrested in Hawaii in late 1999 for crossing state lines in possession of illegal drugs, Hosoi could have—and for all intents and purposes should have—received 120 months in federal prison. Instead, on September 10, 2001, as the rest of the world lay its head down on the eve of one of the darkest days in American history, Hosoi was extended mercy.

"Looking back it was the most awesome thing to ever happen to me," says Hosoi. "It was my chance to seek God with no distractions, no responsibilities. I had nothing—no money, no skateboarding. It was me and God. I was the most excited and happiest prisoner there was. I was a prisoner, yet I was free. The scales came off my eyes, and I could see all that God had for me. The Bible says, 'He whom the Son sets free is free indeed.' I was free."

With a name like Christian, a nickname like "Christ" and a trick he invented deemed "Christ Air," you would think Hosoi would have noticed the connection much sooner.

Hosoi got on a skateboard for the first time in 1975 at age seven, and it was love at first sight. He spent every weekend and most weekdays at the Marina Del Rey Skate Park in Marina Del Rey, California. At a time when skateboarding was a relatively unknown sport, Hosoi was hooked. It was guys like Tony Hawk, Steve Caballero, Lance Mountain and Hosoi who ollied skateboarding into pop culture.

"All I wanted to do was go to the skate parks; it became everything to me," says Hosoi. "It became my form of expression. It was a lifestyle, not a sport."

In 1982, at the age of 15, he turned professional at a time when professional skateboarding was at its grass-roots level. As a ninth grader, Hosoi embarked on a journey to balance skateboarding and schooling. And while he began to climb the ladder toward No. 1, he also started using what were then the norm for pro skaters: drugs and alcohol. Over the course of the next several years, Hosoi dropped out of school to continue his pursuit of becoming the world's best. Eventually, he won several events and competitions and became No. 1, battling year in and year out with Hawk for the top spot, eventually drawing the moniker "Christ."

"I was given that nickname because I was the best at skateboarding. To them I was like a god," says Hosoi. "It was no big deal to me. I had no idea. I wore a cross, and I was religious. When I was asked, I told people I was a Christian, but I didn't know what that was—it was my name."

He also invented a trick that was dubbed "Christ Air" for its resemblance to a crucifix. While in midair, Hosoi grabbed his board with his left hand, put his legs straight, feet together and arms out to his side—all before landing back on the board on the ramp.

At 17, he started a booming business, Hosoi Skateboards. All the while, he was strung out on drugs until he decided to stop cold turkey—at least in his mind. "For two years, the drug use affected my skateboarding," says Hosoi. "So at 17, I quit doing hard-core drugs on the spot because I wanted to be the best. So I decided to just smoke weed and occasionally use Ecstasy, acid and mushrooms every now and then. But I quit all the other stuff—so in my eyes I wasn't a drug user."

From a worldly standpoint, life couldn't have been much better for Hosoi in the late 1980s. The popularity of his sport, which he helped launch, hit an all-time high. With prize money from competitions, his own business ventures, and corporate sponsors like Converse, Jimmy Z Clothing and Swatch, Hosoi was bringing in between $25,000 to $30,000 a month. He bought a beautiful new house in the Hollywood Hills, right next to W. C. Fields's estate, and he began his car collection, which included a Harley, a '69 Mustang convertible, a '60 Chevy and a limited edition McClaren.

"With all that pressure of being a professional and being put on a pedestal, you have to grow up very quickly," says Hosoi, who by this time was in his early 20s. "I was doing everything that was so predictable, and I had no foundation in God. I had good morals and was raised well—don't lie, cheat and steal—but I had no foundation in God."

With the start of the Gulf War in 1991, skateboarding took a dip. Street skaters became popular and the market for vert skaters began to dwindle. The money began to disappear, as did the competitions. The market flipped upside down.

So Hosoi hit the drawing board again, and in the span of three years, he started and stopped no fewer than four companies. He sold just about everything he had, including the house and all the cars, and had to start all over. There was no money coming in. Eventually, Hosoi ended up in Huntington Beach, California, where he still lives.

"There was a pool where I could skate, and I instantly fell in love with the area," says Hosoi. There he dabbled with crystal meth, as he began using it occasionally on the weekends.

"After my businesses began to fold, though, I started using more, and in 1995 I started smoking it. That's when I started spiraling out of control," says Hosoi.

The X Games had just burst onto the scene, taking skateboarding to an entirely new level. However, with no money, a worsening drug habit and no vision for the future, one of the world's Top 2 skateboarders was nowhere to be found—unless it was at a Huntington Beach party as he bounced from drug house to drug house.

Hosoi soon had a brush with the law for possession and ultimately had bounty hunters searching for him. They showed up at skating events; Hosoi didn't. They showed up at local skate parks; Hosoi didn't. Everywhere he used to be the main attraction, he no longer visited.

"I was running all around town," says Hosoi. "In order to avoid getting caught, I had to stay out of the public eye—all for a 30-day sentence. I wasn't able to have a career, so I was getting deeper into [the drug scene]. Because of who I was, though, I was able to get drugs for free, and that supported my habit."

Ironically, the habit led Hosoi to the girl, Jennifer, who became his wife and was a key figure in getting him back on the right track. The two had met at a party, and after Jennifer's best friend nearly overdosed, she had decided to quit partying and get right with God.

She began to go to church, and Hosoi tagged along. At the time it was nothing more than a chance to spend time with his girlfriend. A few months later, though, his fast-paced world came to a crashing halt. It was supposed to be just a short trip. Get over to Hawaii, take some drugs, try to make some money and get back. He never made it out of the airport. As soon as Hosoi got off the plane, federal agents, who had been tipped off, were waiting, and Hosoi was looking at 10 years.

"I called Jennifer three days after I got arrested, and she told me to just trust in God," says Hosoi. "I told her, I think I need a lawyer, not God, and she told me to just trust. All of a sudden, I was confronted with reality and heaven. That was the moment I had to stop and think.

"I opened the Bible for the first time in my life and didn't know where to read. Genesis was like Star Trek, and nothing looked interesting until I got to Kings. That sounded like an interesting story. It was where I first got a clue as to who God was and what He was about. That was my first experience with God. I decided I needed to find peace and truth in my life, and began to understand that they only came from Him. It was the same desire I had when I was trying to become a professional skateboarder. Five weeks later, I gave my life to the Lord."

Hosoi was later convicted, and one day before September 11, he was sentenced. He served the next 56 months alone in a prison cell.

"I was glad it happened, because [otherwise] I don't think I would have surrendered all my junk over to Him," says Hosoi. "For a person like me who thought he was going to heaven anyway, because I was a good person, to be told that I couldn't do drugs, sleep with girls or drink alcohol, because that's sin to God—that was difficult. Being in prison was a blessing in disguise, but looking back, I would have paid for it. I would have given my life to have that time and experience with God."

Still with 14 months left on his original sentence, Hosoi was released on June 4, 2004.

Today, Hosoi is a new man. He's a husband, a father, associate pastor, businessman, speaker and evangelist. Oh, yeah, and still a skater. Yet, whereas before his sole passion was skateboarding, now he has a second.

"I learned to love Him with all my heart in that prison cell. I came to the place where I told God I'd give up everything and preach on the corners or in jungles," says Hosoi. "I told Him I'd give it up—my wife, son, skateboarding, everything. Immediately the Holy Spirit spoke to me and said, 'Christian, I gave you those things. Those are My gifts.' Skateboarding is now my platform to get His message out. This generation is hungry for truth and something that is real, something that is honest, hard-core, sold-out and 100-percent committed. That's how I am able to mesh my two passions—skateboarding and serving the Lord."

Through his church, The Sanctuary, a nondenominational church in Huntington Beach, Hosoi spearheads an outreach called the Uprising Tour, which brings together professional skateboarders and a huge multimedia show in order to reach more than 1,500 youth each show with the gospel.

He's also an active participant and speaker in the Luis Palau Festivals and recently starred in a Luis Palau video called *Livin It*, which was produced by Stephen Baldwin. In addition, he regularly speaks at various venues throughout the country.

"I'm an evangelist and preacher and then a skateboarder," says Hosoi. "When I was in jail, I asked God, 'Why didn't You stop me earlier?' And He was saying, 'I need you for such a time as this.' His timing is perfect. I went through what I went through so I could speak into people's lives. I was willing to let God grab hold of me and mold me. As a result, I want to share the gospel with my generation in a relevant way just like the disciples did."

"I played a big part in making skateboarding huge and popular. I helped start the elevation of skateboarding," says Hosoi. "Now, I want to have that same impact for Christ. God redeemed me and reconciled me back to Him and gave me a burning desire and passion to reach people before they go into a situation, while they are in a situation or while they are coming out of a situation. It's everyone from the young who are just beginning to understand, to the old—that's who I want to win for Christ."

Indeed, music to His ears.

KURT WARNER

SUPERBOWL AND NFL M.V.P.

Imagine what it would take to go from grocery store shelf-stocker to Super Bowl winning quarterback, and you begin to get an idea of the incredible journey that Kurt Warner has traveled. Look up the term "rags to riches," and his picture should appear right next to it. In January 2000, the one-time Arena Football quarterback catapulted to the top of the NFL mountain by leading the St. Louis Rams to a dramatic Super Bowl victory over the Tennessee Titans.

After graduating from Northern Iowa University, Warner was promptly cut by the Green Bay Packers. Working in a supermarket to make ends meet, he was then signed by the Iowa Barnstormers of the fledgling Arena Football League. After a few successful seasons, in 1999 he signed on as the backup quarterback with the St. Louis Rams. When an injury to Trent Green forced Warner into the lineup, he took the field and marched the Rams all the way to the Super Bowl, winning the game and taking the league MVP Award along the way. In 2002, Warner quarterbacked St. Louis to another Super Bowl appearance and a second MVP award. However, injuries and the emergence of Marc Bulger relegated Warner to the No. 2 quarterback slot during the next two seasons, and by the summer of 2004 his career with St. Louis drew to a close.

Later that year, however, Warner signed with the New York Giants and his career appeared to be on the rise again, despite the presence of No. 1 draft choice Eli Manning. With Warner calling signals, the Giants sprinted out to a 5-2 season start. But soon afterward, New York slid into a tailspin and the Giants ultimately decided to give Manning the No. 1 job. Warner left the Big Apple in 2005 and signed as a free agent with the Arizona Cardinals.

Despite his career ups and downs, Warner holds two Super Bowl records: the most passing yards and the most passing attempts without an interception. He is also the third highest rated quarterback in NFL history (behind only Steve Young and Peyton Manning), and the most accurate passer in NFL history, with a completion percentage of over 65 percent.

Throughout it all, Warner's faith has never wavered. He and his wife, Brenda, proclaim Jesus Christ whenever they are given the opportunity, and they work tirelessly for charitable causes. In 2001, the Warners created the First Things First Foundation, which sponsors several events each year and assists organizations that help families and children.

WARNER AND PEACE

By Victor Lee

Despite the battles of the NFL life, Kurt Warner remains at peace and still eager to serve his team and his family.

There is no pretense, nothing ostentatious, no declaration that you are about to enter "Kurt's Kingdom."

There is no evidence of Kurt Warner's football career when you enter the home of Kurt and Brenda Warner and their children. This is a home, not a tribute to football stardom. Oh, there might be an NFL MVP award or two and a Super Bowl MVP award tucked away somewhere in an office or library—or maybe it's in a box in the garage. Wherever it is, it's not in the living room or the media room or the kitchen.

It's not the centerpiece because it's not, well, the centerpiece. Family is foremost, as evidenced by the close-up shots of the children and their parents that fill the living area.

The Warner home might look like yours, give or take a few thousand square feet and the Hummer in the driveway, but even it declares the motto that Warner reinvented on a magical Super Bowl Sunday a few years ago: "First Things First."

There are teenagers and toddlers crisscrossing the carpet, homework waiting to be done, toys strewn about, phone calls to answer, and a tired daddy coming home from work to a loving family and a note from his wife telling him he's a champion. There are joys and challenges. There is—believe it or not—normal life perhaps not totally unlike it might have been had Kurt never made it out of the Arena Football League not so many years ago, when he met and married Brenda and then adopted Zack and Jessie.

It might be very hard to sell most people in middle America on the idea that the Warners are just like them. And, in fact, that would be a lie—they make more money. But, really, that's about it. Their ups and downs—and don't think that stardom offers only ups—are often played out in the media, something the rest of us might like for an hour and hate for a lifetime.

"Yesterday was an awful day," Brenda says, as she sits in the living room waiting for Kurt to come home a day after his worst performance in a long time. "So on the way home, he wants to vent. Say what's wrong with everything, what he could have done better. I don't like football, I couldn't care less about it, and he knows I know nothing and that I'm not coming back at him with a football answer. So I listen. That's what he needed then.

"Then he comes home to the kids. They know nothing about [football]. They don't care how he played. Kurt walks in the door and it's 'first things first.' Those kids cherish him, and they just want to love on him.

"What more perspective do you need?"

That's normal life—joyous, challenging, loving life with its ups and downs totally unrelated to football. To the Warners, life is larger than football; football is not larger than life. Football is business. It's pretty neat some Sundays, pretty crummy on others.

Like the day before the visit to his home. And the day after, when the media crowded around the locker of No. 1 draft pick Eli Manning—the man Warner mentored during his time with the New York Giants—asking questions about when Manning would take over.

"Football is so much of 'What have you done for me lately?'" Kurt says.

What the Warners have done "lately" doesn't offer enough perspective—you need the big picture. Let's be honest about this whole Kurt and Brenda Warner story: It's absurdly, ridiculously unbelievable. Can't you see the young wannabe-novelist approaching the old curmudgeon publishing house editor with his hot new plot: small-college quarterback doesn't make it, stocks groceries, turns to minor league football, meets divorced mother of two, marries and becomes two-time NFL MVP? "Right, kid. Try technical writing."

But it's true. Warner came out of Northern Iowa without any great prospects for pro success. Brenda married, had two children and then divorced; her older son, Zack, suffered a brain injury in an accident. Brenda and Kurt met at a club. They dated four years. He played Arena League ball and was a stock boy for a while. Brenda was a Christian; Kurt was a nice guy who answered "it's between me and God" if asked about his faith.

Brenda's parents died in a tornado, and about the same time Kurt trusted Jesus as Savior. Kurt and Brenda married in 1997. He made the St. Louis Rams as a backup in 1998. Trent Green went down as the starter in the 1999 preseason, and many considered the season lost before it had started. Kurt Warner then led the Rams to the Super Bowl and the first of his two NFL MVPs.

"We're a perfect example of two people who never should have been where we are," Kurt says. "We're also a perfect example that if you put things in God's hands, He can do the impossible."

God repeatedly proves His creativity, His presence and His purpose in our lives by doing in us what no man could think to do. As Brenda's favorite verse, Ephesians 3:20, says, God is able "to do immeasurably more than all we ask or imagine, according to his power that is at work within us."

Brenda says, "I dream big, but I didn't think of this. I always had a testimony before I met Kurt, but no one ever asked to hear it. Then, boom, I had to tell people I don't have time to tell my testimony."

The Warners' testimony covers the ups and downs, the ebb and flow of life, from heart-breaking tragedy to the Super Bowl win. The up times bring the most attention. The down times teach the most lessons.

After three seasons of profound success, Kurt the quarterback fell on hard times in 2002 and 2003. His quarterback rating fell to 69 over those two seasons after averaging 103 the previous three. He was replaced by Marc Bulger and later released by the St. Louis Rams.

The turn of events would crush the spirit of some. While Kurt hasn't enjoyed the struggles, he does see God's hand in it. "I think the greatest thing I learned in life as a Christian is that you have to be consistent," Kurt says. "God's consistent in everything. It doesn't matter how high or how low I get, whether I'm sitting on the bench or stocking shelves, God's the same."

Kurt knew God was teaching him, and he knew the spotlight was relentless. "I always thought I could never be more effective than when I was standing on top," he says. "I thought I'd never have a chance to proclaim Jesus more than in those times. But I found out, being on top and bottom, that God can work when I'm on top and when I'm on bottom—that I'm just as powerful in each situation.

"When I was going through struggles, I can't tell you how many people came up and said that my life was speaking to them more in that circumstance than when I was thanking Jesus on the podium at the Super Bowl. They came to understand that this faith thing is about every single day, not just when things are going well.

"Life as a Christian is about living every day for Jesus, in and despite all circumstances. That's what I learned. Despite the things that may not seem that they're working in my favor, God is blessing me and my family in those circumstances."

The circumstances included repeated finger, hand and thumb injuries. It would be easy for Kurt to blame most of the on-field struggles on those, but the high road is the Christlike road, so he begs off the excuses. "I first hurt the thumb in the first game of the Super Bowl season [in 2001]," he says. "I played all year with the thumb injury. As soon as we lose a few games, they want to jump on the hand-thumb injury, forgetting it was okay when we were winning. It's been interesting from that standpoint. 'What have you done for me lately?'"

Before the 2004 preseason began, Warner signed as a free agent with the Giants. Despite the two difficult seasons with the Rams, he entered the 2004 season as the highest-rated NFL quarterback ever.

But "what have you done for me lately" doesn't count three years back—that's like dog years to human years. Eli Manning was the team's first pick, the golden arm to carry them into the future. Warner was insurance, tutor, short-term starter, or some combination thereof, depending on a person's point of view, which could change with each performance.

Warner won the job during training camp in 2004, but Manning's presence and the media's response left the perception that Warner's hold was tenuous. Eventually, Manning did take over the starting role.

How might that affect his role as Manning's mentor and nurturer? No more than it did when he gracefully helped Bulger, the man who took his job in St. Louis. "A lot of people think I should keep some of my secrets because he's trying to take my job, but I never really approach it that way," Kurt says. "I think it's a great challenge and responsibility to be put in a position to mentor someone in any regard."

That requires suppressing the ego. Though no one does it perfectly, that is part of the call of a Christian—selflessness, others first, a big-picture view.

"I look at my kids, and I want them to be all they can be," Warner says. He explains that he took the same approach with Manning. "I want him to be all he can be. I think it's a great responsibility to mentor beyond the Xs and Os, including the character standpoint, how to carry yourself, how to live in the position and how to represent Jesus in those situations," he says.

It's all about living with the long view, with the intention of making an impact off the field more than on it. Warner has a clear picture of how he wants his teammates to think of him. "I want them to go away saying, 'I played with a great football player, but more importantly I played with a great man, somebody who represents himself the way I want to represent myself.' I hope that they can go away and watch the way I went about practicing every day, the way I went about dealing with my kids and my wife, and that they leave whatever time we had [together] with a great deal of respect for who I am and what I stand for.

"I would love to influence them to believe the way I do, but I don't know how realistic that is. But I hope they remember what I talked about, and that they have a better understanding of who Jesus is to me."

To get an understanding of who Jesus is to someone, you simply watch his or her life.

"I think that Kurt's testimony, along with my testimony, touches so many people's lives," Brenda says. "We've had tragedy and divorce. He's adopted the children. We've been poor and been rich. It's like the full spectrum. If people look at our lives, they are able to identify somewhere along the line. They won't see perfect people, but they'll see two people doing [their] best for God."

BETSY KING

ALL-TIME LPGA LEADER

The Reading, Pennsylvania, native may not have the media acclaim and endorsement allure of an Annika Sorenstam or a Michelle Wie, and she has never been invited to compete in a men's PGA Tour event, but Betsy King has gained plenty of notoriety during an LPGA career spanning three decades and culminating in a spot in both the World Golf Hall of Fame and the LPGA Hall of Fame.

During an impressive career, King was a three-time Rolex Player of the Year and a two-time winner of the Vare Trophy—given to the LPGA player with the lowest season-ending scoring average. In 2006, she was unanimously selected as captain of the 2007 U.S. Solheim Cup Team.

One of the LPGA's all-time leaders in career earnings, King now plays a limited Tour schedule, while serving on the National Board of Trustees for the Fellowship of Christian Athletes and keeping active in the LPGA Christian Fellowship group.

King is one athlete who uses her career success to make a difference in the world. In 2001, she helped organize an LPGA-wide effort through World Vision to raise nearly a quarter of a million dollars for a village in Tanzania; and in 2006, she visited the African nations of Rwanda, Zambia and Kenya, with World Vision. Her involvement with World Vision and other charities, such as Habitat for Humanity and the Christian Children's Fund, serves as an inspiration to her fellow LPGA golfers, as well as to golfers worldwide.

What drives King to such lengths to help others? The answer is simple: her need to follow God's calling. While her pro golf career was certainly part of His plan for her life, it wasn't the whole picture, and she continues to follow His leading with passion and drive.

WORKING-CLASS KING

By Mike Sandrolini

Getting into the Hall of Fame was hard work, but Betsy King isn't resting—she's busy helping people.

Betsy King is glad she doesn't have to answer any more "When are you going to make the Hall of Fame?" questions.

"It's made it easier to come out and play," she says. "I hate to say it, but it was just more of a relief than anything when it happened. Not that it was controlling my life, but there wasn't a day that went by that somebody didn't mention it to me."

"It" was her year-and-a-half long quest for LPGA victory number 30, the total wins needed to earn a place in the women's golf Hall of Fame. The big win finally came June 25, 1995, when King stroked a 9-under-par, 54-hole total of 204 at the ShopRite LPGA Classic in Somers Point, New Jersey.

"Obviously, I can't be living and dying by whether or not I get into the Hall of Fame," King says now about the pressure fans and media alike put on her as she sought that thirtieth win. "[I knew that] if I never get into the Hall of Fame, I still have to live. But people around you tend to build it up."

King isn't speaking flippantly here. She has seen people half a world away living without much at all—let alone having a Hall-of-Famer prefix before their name—and that helps put things in perspective.

At the end of both the 1993 and 1994 seasons, King accompanied a group of LPGA players to Romania, where the women assisted an orphan relief organization. Barb Thomas, Barb Mucha, England natives Suzanne Strudwick and Alison Nicholas, and Jackie Gallagher-Smith each made the trip twice with King.

"We visited several orphanages," King explains. "We were there only a week, but it was more to support some missionaries who were there. Each year we've gone over there not really knowing what we were going to be doing.

"The first year [1993], we went to different orphanages and played with the kids. There was one orphan who was being adopted by a couple in the United States, and we ended up spending a couple of days with him. Last year [1994] when we went, we did a lot of singing. There were nine of us who went, and we sang in front of a couple of different church groups."

The golfers discovered that living conditions in Romania were far from a country-club atmosphere. Even though the former hard-line Communist state has enjoyed a democratic government since 1990, King says the government has been corrupt, and Romanians were still feeling the ill effects of Communism.

"You see a situation like that and it definitely seems more hopeless than it does here in this country," she says. "Like having the government working against you so much. I know people think that sometimes here, but it's not nearly [to] the extent that it is over there.

"I wasn't sure what to expect the first year we were there. The house that a couple of us were staying in didn't have indoor plumbing. It had a shower, but they had an outhouse in the back and there's eight inches of snow out on the ground. That was a little bit unpleasant, but we get so spoiled here in this country in terms of the comforts we have. You go anywhere and it's not going to seem as nice in that respect."

Yet she and her golfing partners relished their time in Romania, and they developed a deep appreciation for the people and their unwavering faith, despite the hardships of everyday life.

"A lot of people there have a strong Christian faith," says King. "They do have more religious freedom than they had before, and that's probably a major difference for them."

"It a real eye-opener," adds Thomas. "Those people literally have nothing, yet they have such a joy of the Lord that we can't even hold a candle to it. Every day they are trusting in God for their provisions, for their safety.

"Even though you just met them for the first time and might not be able to speak their language," says Thomas, "because of that common bond that you have with them of being believers in Jesus Christ, you just feel that you're knitted together. It was quite an experience."

Another new off-the-course experience for Betsy King has related less to packing and unpacking and more to learning how to use the business end of a hammer. In what has become an annual goodwill project at the end of the Tour's domestic season, a number of LPGA golfers put down their clubs, pick up saws and nail guns, and work as volunteers building houses for Habitat for Humanity.

The LPGA's involvement in Habitat for Humanity has grown because of an effort first spearheaded by King and other golfers in the LPGA Christian Fellowship to encourage tour-wide participation. In addition to laboring for the cause, in recent years, King and her LPGA colleagues have donated rounds of golf to raise funds for Habitat, as well as personal items and memorabilia, which are then auctioned off on eBay. The money generated from those auctions goes to fund Habitat projects.

The end result is worth all the effort, in King's eyes. King recalls a specific Habitat project in which she and several golfers built a home in Guadalupe, Arizona, during the 1990s. They later attended the home's dedication ceremony and watched as a family that had once lived in a shack moved into a new home.

"The sister had a trailer and allowed her sister [and her family] to have this plywood shack next to it," says King. "It actually burned down, so they moved into the new home earlier than they were supposed to, before it was finished, just because they didn't have anywhere to go. We've made a difference, I think. Obviously, you don't change the world, but you try to change the world you're in."

Onetime LPGA colleague Robin Walton claims that the Habitat for Humanity project wouldn't have caught on in LPGA circles without King's efforts. "The thing that really strikes me about Betsy is once she gets a goal or an idea in mind, nobody pursues it as hard as she does," says Walton. "She wanted to see the Tour get involved in the Habitat for Humanity project. She really pushed for it. I don't think I could have made it happen the way she did. She really throws herself into something hog wild.

"That's her greatest attribute and her greatest talent. Her tenacity. She gets on to something, and she really wants to see it all the way through."

In addition to the Habitat projects and the trips to Romania, King is involved in several pro-am tournaments for charity throughout the year and contributes financially to help various ministries.

Even though King is eager to serve, that doesn't mean she agrees to every request for her time at charity and ministry-related activities. "Someone told me that in a year's time Billy Graham had 500 invitations to speak, and each one said, 'God told me that you're gonna speak for us,'" says King. "There is always a need, but you can't do everything."

A small-group study in which King participated along with a few Tour members taught her to "find God at His work and join Him in His work. Not, 'What am I gonna do for God,' but 'God, What do You want me to do? Where are You working and how can I help?'

"He'll place that desire in you and He'll lead you where you need to be," she says. "You don't need to be running willy-nilly doing everything. It's very comforting to know that."

Betsy King may not be doing everything, but she's doing plenty to help others. Enough to give her both a Hall of Fame golf career and make her a hall-of-fame person.

JERRY SCHEMMEL

VOICE OF THE NUGGETS

In July 1989, Jerry Schemmel, then the deputy commissioner of the Continental Basketball Association, did something he had done many times before. He boarded a flight from Denver to Chicago. The plane never made it . . .

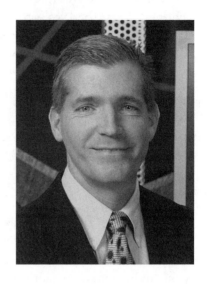

As a horrified nation looked on, United Airlines flight 232 suffered a complete loss of three hydraulic systems and plunged in a fireball into the tarmac of the Sioux City, Iowa, airport. Amazingly—due only to God's grace and the heroic efforts of the crew and rescue teams—175 of the 285 passengers and crew survived, including Jerry Schemmel. Schemmel assisted others around him to escape the burning wreckage, and even rushed back to the flames to pull an 11-month-old baby to safety. Unfortunately, Jerry lost his boss—and best friend—in the tragedy.

Months after the accident, Schemmel was still struggling. It was then that he had a breakthrough—or rather, God did. Schemmel began to seek intimacy with the Lord, who in turn began to bring peace and joy back into his life.

Now a nationally known motivational speaker, Schemmel wrote a book about the ordeal titled *Chosen to Live*. He has been a guest on programs such as *The Oprah Winfrey Show*, *Regis and Kathie Lee*, *48 Hours*, *The Hour of Power*, *The Today Show* and *Good Morning America*.

In addition to having served as deputy commissioner and general counsel for the CBA, Schemmel, a licensed attorney, was also an announcer for the NBA's Minnesota Timberwolves and served as director of marketing (and "the voice") of the Kansas City/Topeka Sizzlers.

During the summers of 2003 and 2004, Schemmel rode a bicycle across the United States as a fund-raiser for two Denver-area charities. Today, he lives with his wife, Diane, and their son and daughter in Colorado; and he continues to board flights as one of the NBA's top play-by-play announcers for the Denver Nuggets.

SURVIVOR

By Gari Meacham

*Nuggets play-by-play announcer Jerry Schemmel is a survivor—
both physically and spiritually.*

From his broadcasting booth at McNichols Arena, Jerry Schemmel, TV and radio play-by-play announcer for the Denver Nuggets, looks and sounds smooth. Well-pronounced words create an even flow to his phrases, which seem confident and assured.

And why wouldn't he sound that way? Surely nothing happening down on the floor can ruffle a man who has been through what he has endured.

It was a crystal-clear July day in 1989 when Schemmel, then deputy commissioner of the Continental Basketball Association, and his friend Jay Ramsdell, commissioner of the league, were assigned the last standby seats on an aircraft that was scheduled to take them from Denver, through Chicago, and on to Columbus, Ohio, where the CBA's draft of college players was to be held.

It would be a short trip—all they had to do was iron the kinks out of a TV-production package and make sure the draft went as planned.

When Schemmel and Ramsdell arrived at the airport for their early flight, they saw "canceled" on the board and were forced to set a different course to get to Columbus. After a frustrating 6-hour wait for another flight, they finally found themselves on board an eastbound plane. Schemmel remembers one of the flight attendants telling the two men as they boarded the aircraft, "I hope you guys don't plan on getting any sleep on this flight. There are a bunch of families with us today with lots of kids, so good luck trying to get any rest."

"Are you kidding?" said Schemmel. "We're just thrilled to be on the flight." That was especially true for him, since he had been the last person booked on the aircraft.

United Flight 232 was packed because of the previous cancellation, and Schemmel and Ramsdell were not seated together. "When I plopped down in seat 23G," recalls Schemmel, "the thought occurred to me that I'd never been happier to sit down in an airplane in my entire life."

An hour into the flight, though, every feeling of relief drained out of Schemmel when a loud noise startled the passengers. "The sound seemed to come from behind me," Schemmel remembers. "Short, but thunderous. It echoed through the cabin with a shock, both physical and emotional, that caused me to bolt upright in my seat. People began to scream, and the idea hit me that not only was I going to die, but all of us in the aircraft were tumbling toward the end of our lives."

The number 2 engine of the DC-10 had exploded, causing complete hydraulic failure. As a result, the pilots had virtually no control over the plane. After the captain announced this mortifying news over the intercom, the flight attendants frantically began to prepare for an emergency landing—giving instructions about how the passengers should brace for impact and exit the plane once it came to a standstill.

"Crying still echoed around me," says Schemmel, "but it seemed softer. I prayed, thanking God that my wife, Diane, was not with me. Then I began to take inventory of my life. I had wonderful parents and siblings, and a great marriage to a woman I adored. I had worked my way through college and law school, and landed a job with the CBA. I had done it all without compromising myself and without cheating or hurting anyone else in the process. 'Take me, God, if you have to,' I quietly prayed. 'I'm ready.'"

Captain Al Haynes flew the crippled aircraft by using engine thrust—an unprecedented procedure. With no steering or brakes, the crew made arrangements with people on the ground to land the plane in Sioux City, Iowa, on a runway surrounded by cornfields.

As the plane dropped toward its uncertain fate, Haynes gave the passengers a final message. He explained that he would give the command "Brace! Brace! Brace!" thirty seconds before touchdown. And he added, "Folks, I'm not gonna kid anybody. This is going to be rough."

As the command to brace came from Captain Haynes, Schemmel could sense that this would be much worse than a crash landing—he was in an airplane that was simply falling out of the sky.

At 4 P.M., minutes after the explosion of the engine, the DC-10 hit the runway.

"It's hard to describe the impact," says Schemmel. "For all the painful clutching of the seatback in front of me, my hands immediately lost their grip. My head, wedged against the same cushion, popped straight up. The irresistible momentum moved me forward and upward from my seat until I had the sensation of floating in air, held only by my seatbelt. I reached out to brace against the seatback in front of me. My hands groped in the darkness but felt only a void. The seat in front of me was gone."

As Schemmel struggled against the laws of physics, the section of the plane he was in flipped over and slid upside-down to its final stop in a cornfield. "I was still upside down when the plane came to rest," says Schemmel. "The next moment I was standing up, with no detailed memory of how I had managed to unbuckle the seat belt and ease to the floor—which was actually the roof of the cabin."

The chill of seeing passengers wandering around a dark cabin, while others, dead, sat still strapped to their seats, would be the first glimpse of what later tortured Schemmel in repeated nightmares.

"I tried to gather my wits," says Schemmel. "I told myself to concentrate on one task—help the others—and perhaps in the process I could find a way out."

People were moving toward an opening in the fuselage. It was an unplanned but welcome exit. While helping those he could, Schemmel made his way toward the opening and exited into the Iowa landscape.

After taking a few steps away from the airplane, Schemmel heard a muffled cry from inside the wreckage. It was the cry of a baby. He quickly headed back into the plane to see if he could find the child.

"I kept moving until I seemed to be standing right over the cries," says Schemmel. "Feeling the floor in front of me with my hands, I realized the child was buried beneath the debris. I reached into a hole, which I would later guess to be an overhead storage compartment, grabbed an arm and lifted the child out. I pressed the child's head against my chest and stepped back out onto the cornfields."

After running from the wreckage to an area where a few survivors sat, Schemmel handed the baby to a young woman. "Would you please take this baby?" he said. "I don't know who she is or where her family is. I just grabbed her from the plane."

Minutes flowed into hours. Schemmel's thoughts turned toward the rescue team that had helped him to safety, to phone calls to Diane and to his parents, and to Jay Ramsdell's parents. Where was Jay? Was he alive, or had he died like so many others? Schemmel would later find out that Jay, along with 111 other passengers, had been killed in the accident.

Although Schemmel left the crash with injuries that were manageable, the months following the crash proved his life was unmanageable. Post-traumatic depression raged within him. Nightmares persisted, and Schemmel was consumed with grief and confusion as he begged God for answers to seemingly unanswerable questions.

The following 10 months held more pain as Schemmel quit his post with the Continental Basketball Association. Although he returned to work a week after the accident, and even filled in as temporary commissioner, he wasn't happy. He couldn't seem to go back to a career tied to the grief of losing his good friend Jay Ramsdell.

Struggling with his difficult transition back to normalcy, Schemmel consulted a counselor who specializes in treating survivors. While talking to her, he discovered that he was suffering from depression. He couldn't work or wish his way back to the way he wanted to be.

"I had gone from successful sportscaster and sports administrator to being a mental patient," says Schemmel. "Guilt, anger, injured pride over my unemployment, uncertainty about the future, a growing sense of meaninglessness about life—they all crowded around me until the despair I felt hung around my neck like a great stone weight."

One night, in the pit of despair, Schemmel shared with his wife, "I'm having a real tough time, honey."

She told him, "I get my strength from God," and left the room.

In the moments that followed, Schemmel realized there was more to a relationship with God than going to church on Sunday and offering emergency prayers as a troubled plane plummeted toward destruction. Schemmel closed his eyes, bowed his head and offered up a prayer. "God, for the first time in my life, I admit that I've been defeated. Please come into my life and help me, because I can't do it on my own. Just come into my life. Please."

Although his life didn't change overnight, a sense of calm began to replace the heartache. "I began to read my Bible daily. I replaced a distant God with a personal relationship with Jesus Christ," says Schemmel. "I read everything I could get my hands on. I studied with my wife, and we attended Bible studies at our church."

With a new sense of hope and direction, Schemmel began to tackle his need for employment. He landed a job on a Denver radio sports show doing morning reports and a midday call-in program. After only two months with the station, Schemmel received a call from the Minnesota Timberwolves, who were looking for a play-by-play announcer. Schemmel accepted the offer, and his career with the NBA began.

Shortly after Schemmel broke into the league with the Wolves, an opportunity opened up for him in Denver. It was a chance to be back in the city he and his wife loved. Full of hope, they headed home. "I love my job," says Schemmel. "I am extremely content where I am."

But being a part of the team has a price. For Schemmel, that price is airplane travel. Basketball teams generally travel from city to city for quick one-night stints. Before they can even unpack, it's off to a new city to play a new team. "Every time I walk down the ramp to an aircraft, I think about it," says Schemmel. "Sometimes I worry that if we hit bad turbulence, I might have a panic attack. But I know God is in control of my life. My faith in Him outweighs my fear."

Jerry's humble attitude and faith may seem misplaced in the arrogance of sports, where some athletes think themselves invincible. "What I went through was so overwhelming that I just wish some guys could see that the craziness of the sport is so shallow. There is so much more in life that is important."

For a broadcaster whose well-chosen words are the platform of his career, Schemmel considers his life—and his purpose for being here—with utter simplicity. "The real reconciliation of the tragedy and the miracle that was United 232 happened for me exactly 10 months after the crash, in the dim light of a bedroom as I sat slumped in a chair," says Schemmel. "It was when Diane spoke the words that were my turning point. The real reconciliation of Flight 232 was giving my life to God."

MARIANO RIVERA

ALL-STAR CLOSER

Believe it or not, the best closer in the history of major league base-ball was originally signed for just about what a good shift manager earns at McDonald's in a month . . .

In 1990, a scout for the New York Yankees just happened to be attending a game in Panama when Mariano Rivera, the 20-year-old shortstop for Panama's Oeste team, volunteered to pitch for his club. Rivera threw effortlessly that day, easily clocking more than 80 mph on the speed gun. Impressed, the scout offered Rivera a contract with a $2,000 signing bonus—and the rest is history.

How ironic that the Yankees, a team known for spending millions in salaries to secure players, initially invested mere pocket change in a man who would eventually become one of the all-time greats.

Even the stats of Hall of Famers such as Rollie Fingers, Dennis Eckersley and Bruce Sutter can't compare to those of Mariano Rivera. As baseball's all-time leader in postseason saves and earned run average, Rivera has been an integral part of four Yankees World Series championships during his career. His best playoff perform-ance arguably took place during the 1999 World Series when the Yankees swept the Atlanta Braves. Notching two saves and a victo-ry, Rivera was named Series MVP.

In July 2006, Rivera, a four-time winner of the Rolaids Relief Man of the Year Award, added even more to his legacy when he became only the fourth closer in history to log 400 career saves.

But saves on the mound aren't the ones Rivera is most preoc-cupied with. Sure, he loves the game and his job, but his love for the Lord rivals both. On and off the ball field, Rivera's priority is "saves." He knows that earthly success is just a passing thing, while the salvation Jesus brings, well, that's forever!

SAVING GRACE

By Bob Bellone

It's all about saves for baseball's top closer, and Mariano Rivera is seeking both the baseball kind for his team and the eternal kind for others.

Jesus saves. Mariano Rivera loves being His setup man.

Since 1995, Rivera has enjoyed mounds of success preserving victories out of the bullpen for the New York Yankees. Along the way, the sensational closer has been warming up for future save opportunities outside the lines. Perhaps sooner than some would appreciate.

Before the 2005 season, fans debated online whether Rivera would gain entrance to the Hall of Fame in his first year of eligibility. One stated that the Yankees would like their stopper to remain in pinstripes until he surpasses Lee Smith atop the career saves list, "though he wants to go off and become a Christian minister or some such nonsense." Some fans took issue with the remark from an admitted atheist, who couldn't grasp the logic in sacrificing a prestigious record and greater baseball glory for a common ministry.

Rivera is uncertain when he will retire, but he does have an ambition to be enshrined in Cooperstown.

"That's one of my goals, to be in the Hall of Fame," he says. His motivation then becomes clear. "I'm grateful to God for giving me life experiences and for giving me that platform to use for His glory. I love that, but even that doesn't compare to salvation."

Always certain about his pitching approach, the trim right-hander isn't sure how he will deliver the gospel message after he stops tormenting batters with his wicked cut fastball and rising four-seamer. Rivera suspects he might get the call to stay in the game.

"I've had in my heart that when I retire, if the Lord is willing for me to do that kind of job, I would love to work with the minor leaguers," says Rivera, who has a passion for guiding young players from Latin American countries.

"That's my love. That's what I know how to do, to teach them about life and baseball. They come without knowing anything, so I want to teach them about the Word of God, because that will make them better people, better players, better everything."

Rivera was among the first Yankees prospects to benefit from a similar ministry begun by Tampa resident Juan Pinol, who in 1990 was recovering from a shoulder injury that ended his budding career as a shortstop in the Cincinnati Reds organization. "I used to go look for the Spanish people and try to help them out—take them to the mall, help them with English, provide transportation, take them home for Spanish food, then take them to church," says Pinol, who still ministers to players assigned to affiliate clubs in the rookie Gulf Coast League and the Class A Florida State League. "I tried to preach the gospel to them and steer them away from party life."

Among his first contacts was Rivera, who wasn't a committed believer when he arrived from Panama as a wide-eyed rookie in 1990. The pair—whose earliest memories include pooling their limited resources on a bargain for shoes—didn't share a Christian walk until 1994.

Rivera was completing a rehabilitation assignment that spring when he suddenly found himself desperate for relief. The day before he was to report for a Double-A stint in Albany, New York, his wife, Clara, became sick and was hospitalized. The couple also had an infant son demanding attention.

It was time to save the closer, and mercy seemed to flow from every direction. The outpouring of love and concern made an immediate and everlasting impression on the young hurler. "The Lord always provided somebody to help me, which caught my attention because things don't happen like this," says Rivera. "I realized the

Lord wanted a relationship with me. That's when I became a Christian."

Rivera since has searched for chances to notch victories for the Kingdom.

The spring training home of the Yankees and their nearby minor-league complex in Tampa are located within minutes of assorted establishments preying on the sinful desires of men. Foul territory to Rivera. "There are a lot of temptations. You have to know what is worth more," he says. "You put them on a scale— your relationship with God or a woman or liquor or spending time with people you shouldn't be with or in clubs. I think salvation is worth more than all of those things."

Rivera has earned widespread respect at the ballpark by carefully guarding his Christian testimony. Nonetheless, he wishes the "saves" would come as frequently off the field as they do on the hill. "Sometimes I get frustrated because I talk to people, and they don't seem like they want to change," he says. "I always ask myself what else has to be done for them to open their eyes and see. But I realize that it's not me who is going to change the hearts of the people. I have to believe and understand that God is in control of everything."

Rivera finds joy in the early spring, when the home clubhouse at Legends Field is overrun with minor leaguers. Before a morning workout, it is common for young players to gather eagerly around his cubicle for a Bible study in Spanish. Rivera doesn't mind the occasional stares or amused looks cast in his direction from other corners of the bustling room.

"I don't care, because I'm not shy about the gospel," he says. "God never was shy about me, so why should I be shy about Him? I always respect that, and if I get an opportunity, no matter where, I will speak because that's what I'm here for."

Team chaplain George McGovern has witnessed significant spiritual growth in Rivera in the past decade. "I see much more confidence in speaking about his relationship with God to his teammates, the media, whomever," McGovern says. "He's much more of a leader than he was in the 1990s in terms of rallying guys to come to chapel or inviting them to a Bible study."

Rivera doesn't limit his invitations to the team. He has repeatedly tried in vain to persuade a certain beat reporter to attend a Baseball Chapel service. "Maybe someday," he says, "but you know what? The seed is planted. You don't plant a seed and tomorrow it's grown already. It's impossible. We plant the seed, and the Lord will do the rest."

His greatest challenge may be convincing rich and famous athletes they are equally as dependent on God as the souls who worship them from the cheap seats.

Rivera wants everyone to know the score. "I want to be as clear as water, as open as I can be, for people to understand that no matter who you are, no matter how much you have, if you don't have Jesus Christ as your Savior, it doesn't mean anything," he says. "If you die, whatever you accomplished and whatever you have stays and you go. And then what?"

Rivera has shared his faith and wealth in generous portions to needy people from the United States, Panama and elsewhere. Pinol remembers the reaction of Cuban missionaries accepting a gift from his friend. "I thought they were going to have a heart attack when they saw the check. I'm not impressed, because I've seen it every year."

Rivera was born November 29, 1969, in Panama City and grew up dirt poor in Puerto Caimito, a nearby fishing village. He was equipped with the natural tools for baseball at an early age. He crafted the rest from anything remotely suitable, such as his cardboard glove. Tree branches and broomsticks served as bats to whack rolled-up rags bound in tape.

"To me, that was the best equipment. I was happy with everything that I got," he says. "I didn't regret any moment. I loved my childhood, and I wouldn't trade it for anything."

Rivera also embraced the game and played every position to avoid the dreaded bench. A longtime Yankees outfielder and friend has noticed the evidence.

"He's probably one of the best outfielders we have. He's always shagging balls," Bernie Williams says. "He plays all fields. He can go and get 'em.

"He's a natural athlete, but he prepares. He works hard, and he makes sure that his body and his mind are always ready when the time comes to play in a game."

Rivera was a 20-year-old playing for his hometown team one day when its staff ace was getting shelled. God threw open the bullpen door and Rivera charged through. "We didn't have any more pitchers," he says. "I grabbed the ball and started pitching. That's when God used that position to put me where I am right now."

Soon afterward, Rivera was spending a Sunday with his family at a beach near their home. Upon his return, a pair of teammates greeted him with word that a Yankees scout was seeking an extended look at him. A week of tryouts culminated in a modest contract that enabled him to cast aside a job working with his father in the fishing business.

"I didn't want that to be my life, to be the job that I would do to support my family," says Rivera, who had tinkered with the idea of becoming an auto mechanic. "What amazes me is that God knows your heart. He knew that my heart wasn't in fishing. I wasn't looking for baseball either, but He has given me the talent and He uses me that way."

In biblical fashion, Rivera was transformed from an unheralded sandlot product into one of the most dominant pitchers in baseball history. Naturally, he gives God the glory.

"He has given me the talent. He has given me the mentality, the wisdom," Rivera says. "Without the Lord, I wouldn't be here because He provided everything for me. Everything!"

Right off the bat, Rivera began producing some eye-popping numbers. He finished his first professional season with a 5-1 record in 22 appearances, dominating the Gulf Coast League with a stunning 0.17 earned run average. In his only starting assignment, he pitched a seven-inning no-hitter.

In 1995, Rivera finally broke into the majors as a spot starter. He gained notoriety the following year as a setup man for John Wetteland, who capped a brilliant season with four consecutive saves in a World Series triumph against the Atlanta Braves.

"All we played for that year was five or six innings because we knew if we had them beat by a run after six innings, Rivera was going to get them in the seventh and eighth and Wetteland in the ninth," former bench coach Don Zimmer says. "That was probably one of the greatest 1-2 punches that I've ever watched in one season."

Both pitchers were promptly rewarded for their success. Wetteland immediately became a free agent and signed a rich contract with the Texas Rangers. Rivera inherited the closer role.

"He just took over, and he made this team a lot better," catcher Jorge Posada says. "He makes it look easy, but it's really tough what he does."

Rivera is the poster boy for mental toughness.

In 2004, the Yankees were celebrating a playoff series clincher he had just nailed down in Minnesota. As the champagne flowed, Rivera and his wife were led aside and informed two close relatives had been electrocuted in the couple's swimming pool in Panama. Rivera endured an emotional funeral, and then returned to New York barely in time to seal a victory that night in the American League Championship Series opener against bitter rival Boston.

Occasionally, the ace fireman isn't so hot. The Yankees seemed destined to clinch the pennant after winning the first three games. The Red Sox, however, shocked the nation with four consecutive victories—two of them on blown saves by Rivera—to reach the World Series they eventually swept from St. Louis.

"We needed to win one more game," he says. "We couldn't win one game out of four? It wasn't meant to be. It was as simple as that. The reasons why? Only the Lord knows why."

And only heaven knows how Rivera squandered his next two chances to protect leads against Boston in the 2004 opening series at Yankee Stadium. When he did, the press box critics and fans brought heat.

Rivera responded by converting his next 31 save opportunities, a personal best. He also made his seventh trip to the All-Star Game in 2005 en route to a career-low 1.38 ERA.

Never, though, did Rivera take pot shots at the Bronx boo birds. "I don't let things that I don't control affect me," he says. "I cannot tell you what to say or what to do. You control that. If they want to boo me, hey, that's okay. If they want to cheer me, they cheer me."

Shortstop Derek Jeter, another close teammate, applauds that attitude. "They boo everybody," he says. "They booed me for a month, too. That's part of the game."

In the opposite dugout, then-Boston center fielder Johnny Damon—now with the Yankees—and his Red Sox teammates were jumping for joy while maintaining a healthy respect for Rivera. "I know we had some lucky streaks against him over the years, but if he blew a game, he was able to come back out the next night and get the job done," says Damon. "We never felt good facing him."

Manager Joe Torre is convinced he wouldn't have collected four World Series rings without "The Hammer of God," a nickname Rivera cherishes. "We played a lot of close championship games," Torre says. "You play close games; you rely on this guy more than any other player on the field."

Rivera delivered the final pitches in three consecutive World Series triumphs between 1998 and 2000, earning Most Valuable Player honors in 1999. Interestingly, he also found a reason to be thankful for an epic collapse against Arizona in the 2001 Fall Classic.

In Game 6, New York was blown out in a bid to clinch its fourth title in a row.

Then the supremely confident Rivera surprised his teammates before the deciding game by urging them to get him the ball late and put everything else in the hands of God.

"He doesn't really talk that much," Torre says. "He's not one of those rah-rah, let's go guys, but when he speaks, everybody listens."

They did that night. Rivera entered in the eighth inning with a 2-1 lead and allowed only a harmless single while striking out the side. Then came the unforgettable ninth. Rivera allowed a leadoff single by Mark Grace, and then committed a throwing error to set the stage for defeat. Tony Womack tied the score with a one-out double. Rivera hit Craig Counsell with a pitch before surrendering a looping single that broke the bat of Luis Gonzalez and the hearts of the New York faithful.

Rivera, who had recorded 23 straight postseason saves since a painful loss at Cleveland in a 1997 division series, walked off in quiet disappointment. Still, he took comfort in the promise in Romans 8:28: "In all things God works for the good of those who love him."

Rivera wondered what good would come from his meltdown in Game 7 of the World Series. He soon was told the subsequent cancellation of a victory parade in Manhattan prompted Enrique Wilson, his teammate, friend and an evangelistic target, to change his travel plans to the Dominican Republic. The airliner on which Wilson originally was booked crashed shortly after takeoff from John F. Kennedy Airport, killing all 260 people aboard and five others on the ground in a residential section of Queens.

"If we would have won it, he would have been on that plane and his life would have been lost. Not only his life, but his family all together would have been lost," Rivera says. "I always was talking to him about Jesus Christ and he always told me, 'It's not time yet, it's not time yet, it's not time yet. I'm not ready, I'm not ready, I'm not ready.' But you'll never be ready because tomorrow is not promised to anybody."

Wilson, who retired from baseball in 2006, was trying to earn an infield spot with the Red Sox that spring when he was asked how being spared from the doomed flight affected him. "I got a second chance and I thank God for letting me live," he says. "Every day, I try to learn something from the Bible. Maybe in the future I'll be a Christian, you never know, but I need to learn more."

Rivera recalls fellow believers not needing the lofty platform he enjoys to share their faith with shaken New Yorkers in the wake of terrorist attacks in 2001. "That opened doors for a lot of people. Everybody was searching for God," he says. "I saw people on the streets, in the hospitals, everywhere, just preaching. It was something that I wish was the same today, but it's not. It's a shame."

In the aftermath of that disaster, the unfailingly humble Rivera presented the second of his four American League Rolaids Relief Man trophies to the Fire Department of New York. "I save games. The real saviors out there are the firefighters and the policemen," he says. "Those are the ones who put their lives on the line, day in and day out. I just got inspired and shared it with them."

Rivera and his wife are overwhelmed by their blessings from God. "I can't believe it. We're just so grateful for where He has put us," Rivera says. "We were nothing. We're still nothing because everything belongs to Him. Because of that, I'm so thankful for what God has done in our lives.

"And He continues doing things. That's the beauty of putting your heart into the Lord's hands. He will do amazing things with your life. Amazing things!"

CHRISTIE SCHWEER

TENNIS MVP

As a freshman tennis player at the University of Virginia, Christie Schweer's fascination with health and beauty turned a desire to lose five pounds into an eating disorder that saw her drop 30 pounds from her 5' 8" frame and become diagnosed with anorexia nervosa. At severe risk of a heart attack, Christie addressed her compulsions with the help of coaches, professional counseling and her Christian faith—*while* being named most valuable player at UV *two times*!

Christie (now Christie Pettit) has continued to share her amazing story by writing magazine articles, doing radio and television interviews, and speaking to young women's groups. She is dedicated to promoting health and wholeness for women through her work as a counselor, writer and public speaker. She has also earned a master's degree in Theological Studies from Emory University, as well as a master's in Marriage and Family Therapy from the Psychological Studies Institute in Atlanta, with the goal of becoming a licensed marriage and family therapist. As if all that weren't enough, she also helps tutor underprivileged junior high school students and works with single women and their children in homeless shelters.

Tennis remains an important part of Christie's life. Over the years she has worked in a variety of settings as an instructor with children, high school girls and adults, and as an assistant coach for Emory University's Division III national champion women's tennis team. She continues to compete with her mother, with whom Christie has placed second in the National Mother-Daughter Clay Courts several times in recent years.

During the darkest hours of her life, when she was feeling completely empty, Christie discovered a way to fill the void: a living relationship with the Lord. Having found her worth in His love, she was able to turn her life around. Today she seeks to share her story with other women, hoping that they too will seek—and find—their true identity and worth in Christ.

Christie lives with her husband, Peter Pettit, and their daughter, Shea, in the Chicago suburb of Evanston.

STARVING TO WIN

By Christie Schweer with Roxanne Robbins

*Christie Schweer—once tri-captain of the Virginia Cavaliers
tennis team—tells how an eating disorder nearly
ruined her career . . . and her life.*

For the first 16 years of my life, tennis was my complete focus.

Everything I did was governed by my desire to improve at my sport. Along the way, I discovered that success won the approval of others, and it gave me a sense of significance.

Despite my hard work, though, during my junior year in high school at Memorial High in Houston, Texas, I experienced the worst loss of my career. I was ranked No. 1 in the state, and I lost to the tenth-ranked player. It was the first time I had ever lost to someone that far below me in the ratings. I struggled to make sense of what happened and wondered why I felt as if my world had fallen apart just because I had a poor performance.

My doubles partner, Christina, came to my rescue. She helped me understand that I was basing my self-worth on how I performed as an athlete. If I won, I was satisfied with who I was. If I lost, I felt empty and as if my life was less valuable.

Then Christina explained that a relationship with God was the only thing that could give my life an eternal purpose. She explained that a personal relationship with God was possible through His Son, Jesus Christ. By knowing and walking with the God who created me, I could trust His plan for my life and as a result gain my significance from Him instead of from fleeting accolades. When I realized that this was the need and desire of my heart, I, by faith, received Jesus Christ into my life. He filled a void that nothing else could fill—not even tennis!

As I continued to play well in high school, colleges started recruiting me. At one time I was the No. 1-ranked prep doubles player and No. 2-ranked singles player in Texas, and I was rated in the Top 75 nationally. I chose to attend the University of Virginia on a full scholarship and was assured a place on the starting line-up as a freshman.

Tennis helped me find my place at a fairly large university. I was playing well and enjoying my studies and new friends, but I had underestimated the difficulty that accompanied the move from my hometown in Houston to Charlottesville, Virginia. Once again I found myself struggling to gain identity. I wanted a way to distinguish myself from all the other women and my teammates who, unlike in high school, were at least as successful as I had been.

A desire to restore my confidence, along with my perfectionist tendencies, drove me to achieve a higher standard. I put in extra hours on the court in private lessons with my coach. Because our team's practice hours were limited by NCAA regulations, I did additional cardiovascular training during my own time. I started eating better as well. In an effort to lose the few freshman pounds I had gained, I cut down on trips to the all-you-can-eat dining halls and limited the number of desserts I ate.

Prior to this time, I had been apathetic about my eating habits. I had always eaten well, but I ate what I wanted, when I wanted.

But now I was discovering that my new eating habits were bringing me some compliments. People all around me, including my coach and teammates, commented on how good I looked. The attention and approval was what I craved, and the initial weight loss improved my performance. I felt lighter on the court and had more endurance.

In addition, I was pleased with how the changes I made were affecting my life and body. The positive reinforcement I received for my improved body condition drove me to stay on my routine and to add to it. Little by little, what began as a simple plan to trim down and tone up my body spiraled into obsessive eating and exercising habits.

I continued to increase the time and intensity devoted to my daily workouts. I eliminated foods, including meat and cheese, that I thought would make me fat. I became an expert on weight loss by reading all the health and fitness magazines I could get my hands on. I learned the caloric and fat content of almost everything I ate, and I plagued myself with guilt if I indulged in any of my forbidden foods. Small meals and fruit, to keep my blood sugar up, became my staples. With all of the nonfat and low-calorie alternative foods that exist, I could easily get through a day without taking in any fat. My goal was to eat the fewest calories possible while still having the energy to do the things I wanted to do.

Excelling in tennis requires discipline and repetitive practice, so I convinced myself I was doing the right thing. By demonstrating such self-control, I felt powerful. I honestly believed I was taking care of my body because I was eating three meals a day and never allowing myself to go hungry.

However, a healthy diet requires a certain balance of calories, fat and protein—all of which I was lacking. Over time, the law of diminishing returns started to affect my body. After I had burned off all the fat I had before, my body started to metabolize my muscle. My body was breaking down, and my weight was dropping drastically as my muscles disappeared.

What started out as such a positive thing was turning into a nightmare.

By the end of my freshman year, the compliments I had been receiving abruptly turned to concern and disapproval. I was confused. Why had everyone who had been so positive about my weight loss become so displeased? I could not believe how quickly I went from being attractive in the eyes of others to being accused of having an eating disorder.

Prior to leaving school for summer vacation, my coach told me not to lose any more weight. Regardless of his counsel, when I returned to UVA for the fall term, my weight had dropped another five pounds. I looked unhealthy, and my coach decided it was time to do something about it. He explained to me that the athletic department has procedures to follow when an athlete loses too much weight. First I had to go to the student health office on campus and have a full physical exam. After that, I was required to meet with a nutritionist and then a psychologist.

When my coach talked about these appointments, I was somewhat relieved. I was frustrated with people accusing me of being anorexic. I was confident that the doctors would assure me, and all the doubters, that I was fine.

But that's not what happened.

My EKG (electrocardiogram) reading revealed that my resting heartbeat was both irregular and dangerously low. The physician informed me I was at risk for having a heart attack. I will never forget going for a run after that appointment—frightened that I could faint or have a heart attack at any moment.

When I met with the psychologist, I received the final blow. I had answered all the questions honestly. Based on my distorted view of my body image, my resulting behaviors and physiological symptoms, her diagnosis was anorexia nervosa.

I couldn't believe it.

But I was glad someone had cared enough to make me discover the truth. My coach's decision to send me to the doctor had forced me to face the reality of what I was doing to myself. I was no longer being healthy. I was tearing my body apart. The longer a problem like mine persists, the worse it gets. I am grateful my coach had the courage to confront me when he did. And I am thankful for the support he, my parents and my friends gave me during the treatment process.

Still, facing the fact I had an eating disorder was shocking. It was difficult for me to admit it to anyone because I felt I was showing weakness. Perfection was my goal. Instead, I was confessing what I perceived as failure.

Weekly sessions with a counselor and doctors helped me see how distorted my thinking and actions had become. As I examined my life, I could now see how I had let my eating disorder take over my existence. Gradually, through treatment, my health improved and my obsessive thoughts and behaviors diminished. But my heart did not heal emotionally. I continued to wrestle with a desire to gain others' approval by my looks and performance.

That summer I attended a camp hosted by the Christian sports ministry Athletes in Action. The camp is designed to teach college athletes how to apply biblical principles to their lives and athletic competition. One of the main teachings is that our identity should come from Christ and not from anything else, especially our performance. I realized that I had been trying to get my identity from having the perfect body and being in great shape. I had completely strayed from the truth about Christ that I had accepted while in high school.

I had grown far from the truth of God. I was not being honest with Him about my struggles. Although my Christian faith was important to me, I was trying to conform to the world's standards. When I opened my eyes to the status of my spiritual life, I saw I had made an idol out of my obsession with fitness. In order to reconcile myself to God, I had to tear that idol down. I had to put my faith in my identity in Christ and trust that I am loved and accepted by God no matter what I look like or how much I weigh. My self-worth has to come from what Christ did when He died on the cross for me—and not from what I do for myself.

Through reading Scripture, I learned that beauty does not come from the outside. I was proof of this. No matter how thin I got, I never felt truly beautiful. I never felt secure with who I was or how I looked. Seeking a beautiful body in the manner I did only left me feeling empty inside. Trying to conform to the world's standards of beauty caused me to almost destroy myself. My desire to be beautiful was actually a desire to be loved and accepted. That is a normal, God-given desire, but it needs to be filled in proper ways. Only God can meet the deepest needs I have. Popularity is not going to feed my soul.

Anorexia has been the greatest challenge I have ever faced. But God has used it to mold my life in beneficial ways. After the breakthrough thinking that helped me view myself through God's eyes, my eating habits improved tremendously. My obsessive food behaviors faded, and I was able to stop seeing a professional.

Now I can eat almost anything without feeling guilty. I have gained over 15 pounds since I was at my lowest weight. Although I gained this weight in a healthy way, I still fear that I will continue to gain weight. I have alleviated this problem to some degree by not allowing myself to step on a scale, but I think I will always be somewhat vulnerable.

It is important for me to keep my focus on my identity in Christ, rather than determining my self-worth by how much I weigh. Generally I am confident in this truth, but when I feel tired or emotional, I am more susceptible to these dangerous thoughts. I have learned many ways of dealing with this issue, such as studying the Bible or talking to God in prayer. It is so comforting to know that even through the most difficult times in our lives, God is encouraging us, protecting us and loving us.

DOCO WESSEH

SOCCER STAR

Soft-spoken Doco Wesseh let his play on the soccer field do the talking for Judson College, located in Elgin, Illinois. In 2004, Wesseh was named Chicagoland Collegiate Athletic Conference Player of the Year, was a member of the CCAC all-conference first team and also was named an NAIA second team all-American while leading Judson to postseason play.

Early in 2005, Wesseh was drafted by the Virginia Beach Mariners of the United Soccer Leagues' First Division. He ended up playing for the Thunder Bay (Ontario) Chill of the USL Premier Development League, the top U23 amateur league in North America.

It's quite a contrast from the hell-on-earth existence Wesseh endured growing up in his native Liberia. Founded by freed American slaves in 1847, Liberia is one of the longest-established nations on the African continent (its capital, Monrovia, is named after U.S. president James Monroe).

The country was at peace when Wesseh was born in 1979, but civil war erupted 10 years later. As rebel troops closed in on Monrovia on Christmas Eve 1989, Wesseh and other classmates—fearing not only for their lives, but also trying to avoid capture by troops who would then force them to fight—fled from their school to the forests and jungles.

Wesseh would spend nearly a decade living in either jungles or refugee camps—facing hardship, disease and death all around—and ended up being separated from his family for years. The war took its toll on Liberia, one of the world's poorest nations, killing more than 200,000 Liberians.

It is miraculous that this story has a happy ending for Wesseh, who eventually came to America with a Christian missionary family. Just as God's hand had guided Wesseh through 10 years of hell, so too did He lead Wesseh to a new life in the form of a college education and soccer stardom. Still, Wesseh hasn't been changed much by the fame and ease of life—he hasn't forgotten where he comes from. He sees with the eyes of faith that his endurance of hardship has enabled him to keep life—and soccer—in perspective.

FLIGHT

By Mike Sandrolini

After an incredible story of fleeing from rebels in Africa, Doco Wesseh took flight as a Judson Eagle.

It's early Friday afternoon. Judson College—located about 40 miles northwest of the House that Jordan Built, a.k.a., the United Center in Chicago—is winding down after another week of lectures, exams and pepperoni pizza.

The first signs of winter have visited the campus. A dusting of snow blankets Judson's soccer field, where just a few weeks earlier the Eagles men's soccer team was rattling off victories at a rate comparable to those of the Michael Jordan-led Bulls teams of the 1990s.

Soccer goals, with their crossbars face down, are in hibernation. Doco Wesseh—MVP and leading scorer of the Chicagoland Collegiate Athletic Conference, as well as an NAIA All-American—had lit those goals up like Christmas trees in 2004. His 20 goals in 23 contests, his 6 game-winners and his electrifying play sparked Judson to a 23-1-1 mark. The Eagles didn't lose a game until the second round of the NAIA national tournament.

Wesseh's braided locks stick out of his black stocking cap as he takes a seat near the gymnasium concession stand, which will soon be open for business as the women's basketball team prepares to play a matinee game. Popcorn, hot dogs, bottled water and Reese's Peanut Butter Cups aren't exactly the staples of a nutritious diet. But neither are cassava roots, wild fruit, dirty river water and fish from that dirty river. Yet there was a frightening period in Wesseh's young life when he had no choice but to live off the latter menu.

The night before Christmas Eve in 1989, Wesseh slept in the comfort of his home in Monrovia, Liberia, with his mother, father, brother and sister. The next day, however, on Christmas Eve afternoon, Doco and his classmates at Carver Mission Baptist Academy were running for their lives as rebels from the National Patriotic Front of Liberia attacked the Liberian capital.

When rebels entered the Academy that day, Wesseh and his third-grade classmates were told to climb out the windows and run. Terrified, they fled into the forest, thinking that within a day or two, the situation in Monrovia would be resolved, and they could go back to their homes and families. Little did 10-year-old Doco know at the time that it would be 11 years before he was able to relocate his family, which lost contact with him after rebels marched into the city on that fateful Christmas Eve.

Wesseh became a statistic—one of a million refugees in Liberia's bloody civil war that would last a combined 14 years. The youngster was forced to live in the jungles and forests of Liberia for three years, hiding with other schoolmates in order to avoid being captured by rebel soldiers, who would force them to take up arms and fight in the war.

Like any other child, Wesseh just wanted to go home and be with his family. But as the days and weeks wore on, he and the others had to concentrate merely on surviving.

Wesseh cut up abandoned car tires and used them for sandals. He would stick baskets in the river in order to catch fish to eat. He and his mates cut down trees and used the wood for tents, then slept on banana leaves.

Trying to make water drinkable also was a daily struggle. Wesseh describes one method he used to try to filter out as much dirt from the water as possible: "We would use a bucket," he says, "poke holes in the bottom of the bucket, and use a plain cloth and put beach sand in there. We then poured the water in there so the sand would suck up all the dirt and make the water clear, and then boil the water for drinking."

Nonetheless, disease spread through the group. Wesseh says that around 25 to 30 people he associated with over that 3-year period died from malaria, cholera, malnutrition or other diseases—including 4 or 5 of his closest friends.

Death, in fact, was all around. Wesseh still wakes up in the middle of the night with flashbacks to his days in the jungle. "Sometimes two or three times a week," he says.

Shootings. Beheadings. Stabbings. Wesseh saw firsthand the cruelty of war. "I saw a lot of stuff like that," he says.

"I knew what he was telling me was true because one of my best friends growing up was actually a missionary from Liberia," says Judson soccer coach Steve Burke. "What Doco went through for so many years . . . it was a pretty incredible story."

Wesseh grew up in a Christian home. "I remember as a kid I accepted Christ, but I don't think I fully understood what it meant to be a Christian," he explains. But he says he began to understand, as he relied on God to help him through his ordeal.

"I used to pray before we'd go out and look for food," he says. "Someone would pray for us, 'Please, God, provide for us today.' The guy I was with, he would go one way, and I would go the other way [looking for food]. And in the evening we'd have something to eat."

In 1993, Wesseh and the group of young teenagers crossed into neighboring Guinea, and then ended up in a refugee camp. Being in the camp turned out to be a God-send. There, Doco attended a Christian revival group, and he also became friends with some of the camp soldiers. He washed their clothes in the river and did other work, and the guards gave him food and clothes. They also gave him a pair of shoes.

Wesseh put those shoes to good use by playing soccer in the camp. One of the camp guards took note of Wesseh's extraordinary skills—Doco had played soccer as a boy in Liberia—and arranged a tryout for him with Guinea's championship soccer team. Wesseh not only made the team at age 15, but he was also named to the starting lineup.

A cease-fire prompted Wesseh to return to Monrovia in 1996. He searched his old neighborhood and asked people in the community if they had seen his parents, but to no avail. "Nobody knew where my parents were," he says, "so I just said to myself, 'Maybe they passed.' [That is, died.] I just decided to move on."

Wesseh stayed in Monrovia, did odd jobs for food and played soccer. "I always used to pray that I would get acquainted with good people that were going to help me go back to school again," he says. His prayer was more than answered.

"One day I was playing soccer, and at halftime, a lady came to me, tapped me on the shoulder," he recalls. "She said, 'We observed your behavior, the way you behave around the other guys, and for some reason, my husband and I just want to take you in, and take you as a son.'"

Dave and Mary Decker were missionaries from St. Paul, Minnesota, stationed in Liberia. While living with the Deckers, Wesseh returned to school and started playing soccer for a Baptist missions team. He ended up taking the S.A.T. and other college entrance exams, and then applied for college scholarship information. Malone College in Canton, Ohio, gave him a soccer scholarship, and Wesseh eventually traveled to Canton in the fall of 2000.

But earlier that year, God had another miracle for Doco. One day, Wesseh met up with a friend who was delivering relief supplies inside Liberia for the Red Cross. "He saw me and said, 'You know, a year ago I saw your dad,'" says Wesseh. "He was working at a little UN clinic. 'I saw them [Doco's mom and dad] there and even spoke to them. They asked me if I had seen you.'"

Wesseh was reunited with his parents a week later. "My family didn't even know me," he says. "I stood in front of them for 10 minutes. They didn't even know who I was until I told them."

After his freshman year at Malone, Wesseh played for the Chicago Eagles Select squad, a semi-pro Christian soccer team coached by Burke. Doco ended up transferring to Judson the following semester and, well, you know the rest of the story.

Running for his life, watching his friends suffer and die, and managing to survive years as a refugee in a war-torn country gives

Doco a unique perspective on life. "Looking back, I think about two different things," he says. "First, if there was a God, how come I had to go through all this stuff? And then I think, maybe that happened to make me stronger and to make me what I am today. I can withstand a lot of hardship. If I don't have money, I don't worry about it. There are a lot of things I don't even worry about."

TIM SALMON

ROOKIE OF THE YEAR

The Rally Monkey took its place among notable baseball props, such as the Minnesota Twins Homer Hankie, during the Anaheim Angels run to the World Series title in 2002.

Tim Salmon ignited plenty of rallies during his 15-year major league career, which came to an end when he retired from the Los Angeles Angels after the final game of the 2006 season. No rally was more important, however, than one Salmon had a major hand in during Game 2 of the 2002 World Series.

In that game, Salmon belted two homers—the latter a two-run shot, which proved to be the game-winner as the Angels defeated the San Francisco Giants 11-10. The victory enabled the Angels to tie the series 1-1, setting the stage for the team's first Series championship in club history.

Owner of a career .282 batting average, the Angels' all-time home run leader (299) hit 30 or more homers five times during his big league career. His best seasons took place in 1995 (.330 average, 34 home runs, 105 runs batted in) and in 1997 (.296, 33, 129). Salmon missed the entire 2005 season as he recovered from surgery on his right rotator cuff and left knee. However, he made the club in 2006 as a non-roster invitee, and then played in what would be his final year of baseball.

Salmon's production off the diamond is as consistent as the numbers he produced on it. In fact, few in the game are more involved with charitable causes as Salmon. He and his wife, Marci, established the Tim Salmon Foundation, which has helped various charitable organizations over the years, such as Family Solutions and Laurel House—two California-based organizations for disadvantaged youths. Salmon's own charity golf tournament annually raises funds for both organizations.

A past Angels nominee for the Roberto Clemente Award—given each year by major league baseball to one player for humanitarian and community involvement—Salmon was once again nominated by the club for the award in his final big league season.

As you get to know Tim Salmon, you'll find that he spends little time focused on what honors he has or hasn't received, what records he did or didn't break. He has learned that what matters most in life is faith and family.

FOR BETTER OR FOR WORSE

By Craig Massey

Tim and Marci Salmon have faced good times and bad times, but were they prepared for what was about to happen?

It was like getting hit by a Randy Johnson fastball.

When the word "cancer" exited the doctor's mouth, Tim Salmon couldn't duck out of the batter's box fast enough to avoid it. The word hit him right in the pit of the stomach.

The Anaheim Angels right fielder had just learned from the doctor that his wife, Marci, had thyroid cancer.

Tim's grandfather had died of cancer, and the terrible experience had left a stain on his memory. Now the word had invaded his life again.

When Marci's biopsy results came in, the doctor's eyes told Tim something was wrong. When the doctor pulled Tim into a separate room, his fears accelerated. "The minute he said 'cancer,' I didn't hear anything after that," Tim says. "My thoughts were that cancer equals death. I kind of lost it."

Tim Salmon met the person who would become his wife, best friend and soul mate during his freshman year at Grand Canyon College in Phoenix. Marci was accustomed to being around athletes—her brothers played sports and her father was a collegiate baseball player—but there was something different about Tim. He was a baseball player with a football player's physique and a love for poetry.

The two met in a freshman English class and later formed a poetry group. "I got him to do his homework by fixing him dinner after practice," says Marci.

"We were like high school sweethearts," says Tim. In 1989, Tim and Marci were married after his first year of minor league baseball.

When Tim's career took him all across the West in pursuit of his major league dream, Marci was always there. She was there when Tim was named the *Sporting News* Minor League Player of the Year in 1992, and she was there when he was named American League Rookie of the Year in 1993. Marci celebrated every home run and every big win with her husband and suffered through every strikeout and every disappointing loss.

Tim has been just as devoted to his wife. As he developed into a catalyst for the Angels and one of the top all-around players in the majors, he was never accused of putting baseball ahead of his family. Tim, who was shuffled back and forth between divorced parents while he was growing up, made it clear that when family crises arise, his heart is with the No. 1 people in his life.

Such as in April 1997.

The new season was just getting under way. Tim and Marci and their two young children, Callie and Jacob, had just made the annual move from Phoenix to Anaheim when Tim noticed some swelling on the right side of his wife's neck. "It was just the angle I was at with the light hitting it," Tim says. "You couldn't tell any other way."

It took a lot of urging from Tim and from Marci's parents to convince Marci to see a doctor. "I'm not one to go see a doctor," she says now about her reluctance. "I have a very positive outlook. Nothing's going to happen to me."

Finally, wisdom won out, and she met with the Angels' team
doctors. After examining her, they recommended that she set up
an appointment with an endocrinologist. In the meantime, the
swelling disappeared, but Marci decided to keep her appointment with the specialist anyway. On May 20, the endocrinologist
did a biopsy and the results stunned everyone. Everyone, that is,
except Marci.

"The minute the doctor told me it was thyroid cancer, the next
sentence was that it was 95 percent curable," Marci says. "He said
they just take the thyroid out, and it's out of your body and out of
your system. For me, that was enough to hear. I was very much at
peace with it after that. My positive outlook was, 'Fine, great, let's
get it out.' It was like I had appendicitis or something. Sometimes
my naïveté serves me well."

"She's very fortunate to have her dad's personality, and his
personality is not to worry about anything," Tim says. "Everyone
said, 'She's just like her dad. Nothing bothers her.'"

Word spread from California back to Phoenix about Marci.
Calls started coming in from other family members, friends and
members of the church the Salmons attend in Phoenix. The
phone calls usually ended with Marci cheering up the person on
the other end.

To Tim, learning the biopsy results was like finding out that
someone or something was trying to take away the most precious
thing in the world to him. He wanted answers, he wanted facts,
and he wanted them now. The fear of losing his wife weighed heavily on his mind. He thought about how he could cope as a single
father with two small children. He wondered, *Who would take care
of them during the season? Why was this happening? Could this have been
prevented?*

The emotional strain brought Tim to his knees . . . literally.
He took his questions, his burdens, his fears straight to the top.
"There was a lot of soul-searching and a lot of prayer," Tim says.
"This is where the rubber meets the road. I went through the
whole process of questioning everything. I just needed to take a
refresher course in what God is about and the promises He has for

us. I had to kind of rebuild the foundation that all of a sudden was a little bit shaky."

The foundation of Tim's faith in God can be traced back to his college days. Tim accepted Jesus Christ as his Savior shortly after arriving at Grand Canyon College, and his growth as a Christian was helped by the people around him.

When Tim was a freshman at Grand Canyon, senior catcher Acey Martin served as a spiritual mentor to Tim, answering his questions and providing a godly example for him. Playing next to him in the outfield was Chad Curtis, who would go on to be a teammate of Tim's with the Angels and who also was going through growing pains as a young believer. Off the field, Marci and her family gave Tim a clear picture of what a Christian family is all about.

"Coming out of a family where the parents are divorced, I got to see a family where both parents loved each other," Tim says. "It was a Christian home the way God intended. By spending time with Marci, I got to spend a lot of time with her family, and they were very instrumental in the development of my faith and growth."

By the time the cancer diagnosis came, Tim had invested a lot of prayer and hard work in his family. He and Marci loved the Lord, attended church and Bible studies regularly, and were raising their daughter and son to do likewise. There was nothing about losing his wife to cancer in Tim's vision of the ideal family.

"For the first few days, all I could think about was 'What does this mean?'" Tim says. "You're pleading with God, 'Give me an answer.' I hate to say it, but I had all those initial negative reactions."

After the shock wore off, Tim sought out some clear answers from the doctors. Complicating the situation was the fact that cancer had also been found in Marci's lymph nodes. "That was a different concern," Tim says. "Thyroid cancer doesn't usually spread, but we all know what happens when cancer gets in the lymph nodes. It spreads throughout the whole body."

Marci underwent surgery on June 2, 1997. The doctors removed her thyroid gland and then gave her a heavy dosage of radioactive iodine pills to kill any remaining cancer cells. In July the doctors did a radioactive scan, and a there was a "flicker" on the screen when the scan crossed over her chest. A more detailed scan didn't reveal anything. As a precaution, the doctors ordered another scan to be performed in January, six months after the surgery.

Despite the awesome challenges that come with cancer surgery and recovery, Marci maintained her cheery personality throughout the summer. Her story spread throughout Southern California and the baseball community. Strangers would approach her and tell her that they were praying for her. Then came the fan mail. "That just showed me how good God is to have fellow believers reach out to you," Marci says. "It was fabulous."

Tim faced a different set of challenges. There were days when baseball faded into the back of his mind. "For a while my outlook was not the same," he says. "It was important to give my best effort, but you know what, I didn't care if we won or lost there for a while. There are other things to be thankful for and other things that are more important.

"There might have been one or two games where I was really distracted by it," he says. "On the day I found out, I think we were playing Seattle, and there was a lot of excitement and energy in the stadium. But I was like a zombie out there."

The pain and the uncertainty of the ordeal aren't what linger in the minds of Tim and Marci, though. What they took away from the experience is the lasting picture of the outpouring of support from friends, people associated with the church, opposing teams' ball players and even strangers.

Both agree that the experience brought them closer to the Lord. "Maybe it was just time for us to reflect and think about God," Marci says. "Being a Christian doesn't mean you're not going to have problems."

Tim gained a new appreciation for his wife and says God opened his eyes to the joy that's in his life. "I'm thankful that I had the opportunity to have my eyes opened and be enlightened to the joy that is around me and that maybe I take for granted," he says. "I've had to persevere in my life, but it's always applied to baseball. For the first time in my life, I had to persevere in something much more important than baseball. That's what this whole spiritual journey is about—growing in our faith and being more Christlike every day."

On January 22, 1998, the Salmons made the trek back to Anaheim from their home in Phoenix for the six-month check-up and radiation scan. The news was an answer to their prayers.

"Everything's perfect," Marci says. "It was a huge relief. It surprised me how good it felt. Now we can just close the book on this and go on."

AVERY JOHNSON

NBA COACH OF THE YEAR

As Avery Johnson paces in front of the Dallas Mavericks bench, he exhibits the same passion, drive and feistiness that were his trademarks during 16 seasons as an NBA player.

Johnson helped the San Antonio Spurs win the 1999 NBA championship, capping their run to the crown by sinking the game-winning shot in the title-clinching contest. Now, he wants to lead Dallas to the promised land. And if the success Dallas has enjoyed so far under his leadership is any indication, it probably won't be long before he and the Mavs are hoisting the Larry O'Brien championship trophy.

Colorful Mavericks owner Mark Cuban awarded Johnson with a contract extension through 2010-11 after Johnson took Dallas to the 2006 NBA Finals in his first full season as head coach. Johnson also reached two other benchmarks during the 2005-06 regular season. First, on March 16, 2006, he set an NBA record for the most victories by a coach—66—through his first 82 games (a full NBA season). Then, Johnson, a multiple NBA Coach of the Month winner, was named NBA Coach of the Year.

Johnson's will to win, however, pales in comparison to his desire to reach out and help family, as well as his fellow man, in a time of need. A native of New Orleans, Johnson and his wife, Cassandra, used their home in Houston as a halfway house for family members and friends who were victims of Hurricane Katrina. He and his wife also sent money to relatives, and put displaced individuals up in hotels and vacant apartments around Houston.

Additionally, Johnson supports organizations and church programs in Dallas, Houston and New Orleans that reach out to hungry, homeless and underprivileged individuals and families. He's also in great demand as a speaker at churches and schools.

While Johnson shines on and off the court, where he's really impressive is in his walk with Jesus Christ. Whether on the road or at home, he is constantly feeding his soul with the Word of God and seeking to be a light to others. Johnson is a man who walks the talk, reflecting the love of Jesus to a world in need.

WELL-SUITED

By Darryl Howerton

Who knew that this little-known guard from Southern University would turn out to be just right at the helm for the Dallas Mavericks?

Everybody has an Avery Johnson imitation.

His is easily the most recognizable voice in sports, like Howard Cosell was back in the 1970s or Mike Tyson in the 1980s. That's why everyone who has ever played with or observed the man nicknamed Little General has his own impersonation of the high-pitch, highly enunciated Louisiana twang that comes out of the mouth of the energetic 5′ 11″, 185-pound dynamo.

That being said, one thing is clear. No one has ever been able to do the man justice. Because you just cannot duplicate the man. Avery Johnson is an original.

No player's career arc ever ran all over the place—quite successfully we might add—with so little credit, until late in his career, when everybody recognized he was a winner. Not many head coaches ever jumped into the fire at such a young age either, and none ever had the success he's had, as quickly as he's had it.

Immaculately and impeccably dressed in his monochromatic suits on the sidelines, he rivals Pat Riley as the best-dressed coach in the league, and more important, his win-loss record as coach is rivaling Riley and the greatest coaches who ever suited up, so to speak.

In his first two months in coaching, Johnson won NBA Coach of the Month honors both times. And then he rode that surge to become the first coach to win 50 times in just 62 games, breaking the record of 63 set a half-century ago by Red Auerbach and Al Cervi.

"It was a crazy time," says Johnson, recalling his indoctrination in the league. He was a player trying to make the Mavs roster in October 2004, decided to become a Dallas assistant coach in November, and was groomed for the head coaching job during the season when Don Nelson and team owner Mark Cuban decided he was ready for the job in late March 2005.

"I knew I'd be taking over at some point, and everybody thought that would be a terrific time for me to take over," says Johnson. "I had already coached a couple stretches when Nellie was out with health problems. So when I got the job at the end of the season, it just seemed like the right time. I had learned so much from my coaches, especially Coach (Gregg) Popovich and Nellie, who took so much time last season preparing me for the role. When Mark Cuban thought it was a good time, I knew I was ready."

Johnson's Mavs went 16-2 in April 2005. But perhaps the most notable changes among his charges were the newly defined roles they had been given. Nellie had been big on changing lineups, playing small-ball at times, trying to create lineup mismatches—yet Johnson was more straightforward. The year before in the 2004 NBA Playoffs, for instance, power forward Dirk Nowitzki dedicated a lot of his efforts guarding Sacramento Kings center Vlade Divac. With Johnson in charge, Nowitzki no longer guarded centers.

Another area that Johnson was quick to stress was defense and rebounding. He gave Josh Howard and anyone else who played hard D monster minutes, tried to make Jason Terry a leader, and touted Nowitzki as a good defender when the knock had always been on him as being a below-average one.

It was extreme makeover at its finest. The Mavericks already had a winning ball club, perennially winning 50 games a season as often as Kobe scores 30 points a night. But Johnson needed to make them a championship one.

"It was a necessity for us if we want to make that next step," says Johnson. "That's the type of basketball I was taught in San Antonio. We already had an offensive identity in Dallas, but we needed an overhaul defensively. We had to get good enough on defense to compete in the NBA Finals, and the players bought into it."

In the 2005 playoffs, Dallas dropped the first two games to Houston, prompting some to speculate he was being out-coached by Jeff Van Gundy. Johnson's Mavs responded by D-ing up the Rockets, beating them at their own game and winning the round in a seven-game series.

The Phoenix Suns, owners of the NBA's best record that season, ended up beating Dallas in Round 2, but Johnson's point had been made.

And it showed in the 2005-06 season, with Dallas getting off to a great start and maintaining the 70-plus percent winning basketball that kept them among the top three teams in the league all year long, along with the San Antonio Spurs and the Detroit Pistons (winners of the 2004-05 and 2003-04 NBA championships, respectively).

Johnson is especially happy that his Mavericks have challenged his former team, the Spurs, whom his club defeated in the 2006 NBA Playoffs. The Mavs also knocked off Memphis and Phoenix during the postseason, but fell to the Miami Heat in the NBA Finals.

"I just think it's great for basketball," says Johnson of his rivalry with his beloved former coach, Pop, and his MVP former teammate Tim Duncan, who together with Johnson won the Spurs' first NBA championship in 1999.

"It's great for the state of Texas for us to be neck and neck all year long. I've known these guys a long time, so obviously there's a lot of respect for Pop and Tim. That's an NBA championship team there, and that's what we're striving to be."

Life has changed, but it's nice to know that through it all Avery Johnson has not. He's still the same feisty, energetic, God-loving, Jesus-praising man he always has been. He's the same guy about whom teammates throughout the years always said, as Tim Duncan puts it, "Avery was destined to be a head coach one day. Everybody knew he'd do that one day."

His team success—sparked by his leadership—always seemed to follow him in his early journeyman career. Thought to be a perennial "twelfth man" on the roster, the undrafted NBA point guard would bounce from Seattle to Denver to San Antonio to Houston and back to San Anton' and Golden State on 1-year and multiple 10-day contracts his first 6 years—but one fact was nearly unmistakable. Every team Johnson left would resort to its losing ways. And every team he joined would become winners. It was no coincidence.

It also was no coincidence that Golden State named him their team captain in the 1993-94 season after he was on board for just nine days. That's how quickly his leadership qualities became apparent when he joined new teams, despite doubts about his playing ability.

Popovich, then an assistant for the Warriors, took definite note of Johnson's captaincy skills, and when Pop got the general manager job with the Spurs, he made sure he made Johnson his point guard, a tenure that would last fulltime for the next seven seasons.

And though his high-pitched, always-squeaking twang might get under the skin of a teammate or two—because of the constant barking—he never really felt any backlash because of his spiritual beliefs, then or even now as a head coach. "Not really," says Johnson. "People see what happens with me. I just want to be a reflection of Him. Be a light. I don't have to tell people all the time about Jesus. I don't have to hammer them over the head about it. They know I know Jesus, and they respect that."

Johnson's playing career peaked in 1999, when he was the floor general on the NBA championship squad, averaging 10 points, 7 assists and 33 minutes per game for the team led by All-Stars Duncan and David Robinson.

It's no wonder that he's molded his Mavs into some semblance of the Spurs team, right down to the spiritual leadership aspect that made Johnson the player and leader he was . . . and is. Just as Robinson and Johnson led the Good Guy Spurs back in the day, the Mavericks have a strong Christian contingence that gathers regularly.

"And I get a lot of my strength and counsel from Del Harris, who is an ordained minister," Johnson notes. Harris, too, is an ordained head coach, so to speak, with over 45 years in the business. His is the voice that gives advice to Avery's ear.

"You couldn't meet a nicer guy than Avery," says Harris, who has recorded over 500 victories as a head coach with the Los Angeles Lakers, Milwaukee Bucks and Houston Rockets. "And when it comes to coaching, he puts so much time and energy into it. In fact, sometimes it's too much, and we sometimes have to back off. It's true he was put in the ideal situation, but he's done a great job with that opportunity, and he's just going to get better."

It's this close bond with fellow coaches and players that keeps Johnson sane in a roller-coaster year on the job. "Keeping balance spiritually is very important in a very high-energy job like this when the hours are long," says Johnson. "It's pretty mentally draining, but I always find time to pray.

"I make time for it. I'll make sure on the road I have CDs of my favorite pastors. I'll read spiritual books. I'll talk with the chaplains at the NBA chapel service. You have to do this, when you spend so much time on the road."

A quick survey of his current CDs in rotation include sermons from Terrence Johnson of Houston, T. D. Jakes of Dallas and Walter Thomas of Baltimore, while the book in his travel bag is *21st Century Leadership: Dialogues with 100 Top Leaders.*

"I like to have my quiet time in the morning," says Johnson. "That's when I like to pray and be with God. But I never know when I'll listen to a CD or read a book. It makes me feel more at home when I take these with me. I may watch Christian television or pop in a CD and listen to a sermon."

So whether he's on the road, breaking away from game-planning for his next opponent, or at home, where he may be TiVo-ing and watching three games at once, Johnson knows it's his relationship with Jesus that put him in this position . . . and keeps him in this position.

"I am walking the walk," says Johnson. "Everything in life is so spiritual. You can't lose sight of that. But you can't be so religious that you're no earthly benefit. My whole career was making something out of something while facing adversity. Getting cut. Signing with a new team. Over and over. In every situation, though, I tried to be a light. I would outwork and outstudy the best of them. Be a light. Be unselfish. Be a reflection of Him.

"I learned early that I got blessings to be a blessing. That's the same mind-set I have today."

We see it when we see Jason Terry become a team leader. We see it when we see Dirk Nowitzki become a tougher player. We see it when we see Josh Howard become an All-NBA defense player. We see it when the Mavericks play championship-contender basketball.

Avery is a reflection of Jesus. And in turn, the Mavs have become a reflection of Him as well.

MATT HASSELBECK

SUPERBOWL QUARTERBACK

If Matt Hasselbeck happened to be your coworker, and you drew his name for your office's secret Santa gift exchange, finding a gift for him wouldn't be a difficult task. When asked by *Sporting News* to submit a Christmas wish list of five items, among the items Hasselbeck listed were "new headphones to travel with because my daughter broke my other ones" and "Graeter's chocolate chip ice cream from Cincinnati."

Hasselbeck says Graeter's is the best ice cream in the world.

Speaking of good things to eat, chances are the Seattle Seahawks quarterback also stocks his kitchen cabinets with Campbell's Chunky Soup. In 2006, Hasselbeck joined Pittsburgh Steelers QB Ben Roethlisberger and Campbell's longtime Chunky Soup pitchman Donovan McNabb—the Philadelphia Eagles' quarterback—in the soup company's widely popular "Hungry Boys" ad campaign.

Going long for Campbell's isn't, of course, Hasselbeck's forte. He saves his best bombs for Seahawks' receivers. The two-time NFC Pro Bowler helped lead Seattle to four straight postseason appearances (2003-2006), which included an NFC championship and a berth in Super Bowl XL. En route to the Super Bowl, Hasselbeck completed 294 of 449 attempts for 3,459 yards.

Football pedigree certainly is evident in the Hasselbeck family, as Matt's father, Don, played tight end for the New England Patriots. His younger brother, Tim, also is an NFL quarterback. Tim and Matt both were starting quarterbacks at Boston College.

A legacy of generosity applies to Hasselbeck as well. Stories of Hasselbeck taking time to visit with fans he happens to run into off the field are many. Matt also has his own charity, the Matthew Hasselbeck Foundation, which provides financial support to local charitable organizations and helps meet community-wide social, health and educational needs.

Behind all of Hasselbeck's accomplishments is his desire to be all that God has created him to be, both on and off the field. With the help of an unlikely mentor, he came to see that he has been called for a purpose: to make the most of his God-given talent and to seek a deeper relationship with the Giver of all gifts.

THE AMAZING JOURNEY OF MATT HASSELBECK

By Gail Wood

Perhaps you thought Mike Holmgren was the guy who keyed Matt Hasselbeck's success. But the true influence just might be a poor leper in Jamaica.

It was here, in the poverty-torn country of Jamaica, while sitting next to a man grotesquely disfigured by leprosy, that Matt Hasselbeck began his unexpected journey to the NFL, to the Pro Bowl and to the Super Bowl.

It was here, as Hasselbeck watched with amazement a man who had lost his fingers, ears, nose and sight to leprosy joyfully praising God in prayer and in song, that the Seattle Seahawks quarterback discovered the meaning of contentment and commitment.

Ten years ago, Hasselbeck, as a sophomore at Boston College, took a 10-day missionary trip with 16 classmates and Father Ted Dziak to Jamaica. Hasselbeck came back a different man.

"No question it was a life-changing experience," the Seahawks quarterback says.

The trip to Riverton City, a shanty-town built on a garbage dump near Jamaica's capital city of Kingston, gave Hasselbeck a grim, up-close look at desperate poverty—something the son of an NFL tight end growing up in Boston had never seen. On several days of the trip, Hasselbeck worked in a home for elderly lepers.

He cleaned, scraped and then painted a bathroom in the home. In the evenings after a day's work, he'd join the lepers for song and worship. It was then that Hasselbeck met George McVee, the man disfigured by leprosy.

The first evening, Hasselbeck was the last to arrive and only one chair remained. It was next to McVee.

"I'm ashamed to say this, but it was hard to look at him," Hasselbeck says. "I didn't really want to sit next to him. His leprosy was so much worse than everyone else's. They said it wasn't contagious, but I was a kid. I didn't know."

With Hasselbeck seated, McVee held a harmonica between his stumps and played hymns. And everyone sang. There was no other music besides the voices and McVee's harmonica.

In between songs, McVee spoke, reciting long passages of Scripture and poems he had composed. One of his poems he titled "My Cup Runneth Over."

"Then he'd say, 'Thank You, Jesus. Thank You, Jesus,'" Hasselbeck recalls.

And Hasselbeck looked at this deformed man and the others in wonder.

"I said to myself, *These people should be so angry, given what they were born into—poverty, poor health. What do they have to be happy about?*" Hasselbeck says. "But in their eyes, it was the exact opposite. Their attitude was what my attitude should have been like."

After leaving the home for lepers, Hasselbeck spent several days at a Catholic-supported school for children ages three to six. The children wore uniforms given to them by the school. Many of them had no shoes. None of them had eaten before coming to school.

They all lived in homes with tin roofs, no windows, no electricity and no running water. While there, Hasselbeck lived in one of those shanty homes, sharing it with a mother, her 22- and 10-year-old sons, and her grandmother.

One afternoon Hasselbeck was outside this one-room school playing games with the children. Suddenly, a grief-stricken woman clutching her dead son ran toward the school, screaming for help. Her four-year-old son had fallen into a latrine and drowned in sewage.

A nurse at the school tried to revive the child.

Hasselbeck remembers the scene vividly. He remembers the chaos and a sense of utter despair. Overwhelmed by the scene, he vomited.

"We [did a lot of] reflecting that evening," Father Dziak says. "There wasn't a single person who didn't have tears."

A month after arriving home in Boston, Hasselbeck got sick with hepatitis A, which he probably got from drinking the water in Jamaica. He was hospitalized for six days, his weight dropped from 215 to 185, and he missed spring football practice. All 100 of his teammates had to get hepatitis shots.

Jaundiced—his eyes and skin yellow—he lay in the hospital, waiting for his release and wondering about his future in football.

"But I never really thought, 'Why me?'" says Hasselbeck, who was one of four students on the trip who contracted hepatitis. "I thought, *This is nothing compared to what the lepers in Jamaica deal with.* And they had so much joy in their hearts because of the Lord, despite their circumstances."

It was then than Hasselbeck made a promise to God.

"While lying in that hospital bed, I said a prayer," Hasselbeck says. "I said, 'Dear God, I apologize for not using my health and athletic ability You've given to the fullest.' I made a promise that when I got better, and I knew I'd get better, I was going to try as hard as I could all the time."

Whether coaches were watching or no one was watching, Hasselbeck promised he'd always push himself and that he'd always try his hardest. Up to that point, that wasn't something he did.

"I made a lot of excuses why I wasn't playing," says Hasselbeck, who was a seldom-used backup his freshman and sophomore seasons. "All of the time somebody else was the problem. Not me." It was the coach's fault he wasn't starting. Or a wide receiver's fault. Or the linemen's fault.

"I also think I didn't work as hard as I needed to because I think that gave me an out if I wasn't successful," Hasselbeck says. "If I wasn't named the starting quarterback, it was, well, I didn't try that hard anyway."

All that changed with his prayer in the hospital.

After his release, Hasselbeck remembers vomiting after running sprints by himself at a track not far from his home. He was really pushing himself now—striving to realize his God-given potential. "I was doing this for an audience of One now," Hasselbeck says. "I was now playing for the Person who created me. And I was going to make Him proud and to not waste this ability He's given me."

The results were dynamic. He went from being a forgotten backup to the starter.

"I was a terrible player who couldn't even break the top four," Hasselbeck says. "I became the guy who became the starting quarterback, who played well, who made the NFL practice squad with Green Bay, who moved up to the backup spot and who became the starter."

It was a long hard road, directed by one moment. "I really think it all started with that lesson I learned in Jamaica," Hasselbeck says.

Hasselbeck didn't begin the season as the starter his junior year at Boston College. But he came in off the bench with his team trailing Hawaii and led the Eagles to a touchdown and a field goal as time expired for the win. He started the remaining 10 games that season and started his entire senior year to become the school's fifth all-time leading passer and a sixth-round draft pick by the Green Bay Packers.

He had returned from Jamaica with a better appreciation for life and for the things he had. Simple things like running water, a light switch and windows. "When I got back home, I felt so guilty," he says. "I felt guilty every time I brushed my teeth and left the water running. I felt guilty any time I left food on my plate. I felt guilty about complaining about anything."

Hasselbeck had been an unexpected member on the trip to Jamaica. His football coaches at Boston College had objected, saying that making trips like that wasn't why he had come to school. He was the first football player to make the trip, but he wasn't the last. His brother, Tim, now a quarterback with the New York Giants, later followed, along with other football players.

When Hasselbeck had packed his bags and boarded the plane heading for Jamaica, he left with the sense of being a provider. He was going with a mission—to help.

Instead, he got an unexpected surprise. "We all went down there to help them," Hasselbeck says. "We thought we could help them because we had the money and the time. When I got down there, I realized, 'Yeah, we helped them a little. But they helped us.' They helped me more than I ever helped them. I thought I was giving, but I was receiving."

The return wasn't monetary. It was seeing the joy that shined in the lives of people like McVee. "I thought Matt might have regretted going to Jamaica," Father Dziak says. "But he never had a sense that he wished he hadn't gone. You sometimes wonder why God puts you in places or sends you to places. But there was always this sense that he gained so much from it."

After the trip, students who had gone on the outreach wrote their thoughts in a log book. Hasselbeck wrote, "We came down with money, food and supplies to better your lives. You've given back to me a hundred times what I could have given you."

When Father Dziak visited Hasselbeck in the hospital, he asked the future All-Pro quarterback if he regretted going. "He said no and he'd do it all over again," Father Dziak says.

Father Dziak doesn't think fame and wealth have changed Hasselbeck's "God-centeredness." "That's who he is and who he'll always be," Father Dziak says. "Even as aggressive as he is on the field, get him off the field and there's a real gentleness and a real spirit about him—you always feel that God is present there."

Hasselbeck, the oldest of three brothers, was drafted by the Green Bay Packers in 1998 after being a two-year starter at Boston College. He and his middle brother, Tim, met in a game early in the 2006 season, with Seattle beating the New York Giants 42-30.

They grew up in a Christian family and remain very close, often critiquing each other's game. Matt Hasselbeck remembers his parents getting "serious" about their Christian faith in 1982 when he was in second grade.

"We went to church and Sunday School every Sunday from there on out," Hasselbeck said. "I don't have one of those strong conversion experiences—I wasn't a crack addict or something. I was fortunate. I was raised in a home where values were taught."

The Hasselbecks are a football family. Their dad, Don, played tight end in the NFL for nine years, playing for the New England Patriots, Oakland Raiders, Minnesota Vikings and New York Giants. Youngest brother Nathanael played safety and returned punts at Boston College. Their mom, Betsy, even has a football link. Five of her seven brothers played quarterback at Boston.

Before Matt Hasselbeck could raise the NFC championship trophy above his head in January 2006, before he could play in the Pro Bowl, before he could start as quarterback for the Seattle Seahawks, he'd have to meet a blind man who has no fingers, no ears and no nose.

He'd have to meet George McVee.

"People say to me that because I'm an NFL quarterback I'm a role model," Hasselbeck says. "But you know what? Everyone is a role model. Whoever would have thought that some elderly guy with leprosy in Kingston, Jamaica, would be one of the top role models in a 19-year-old kid's life?"

Hasselbeck came back from Jamaica a different person. He was committed to a game and to God, less likely to hide behind excuses. And he was determined to make the most of his talent.

During the Seahawks' ride to the Super Bowl in 2005, Hasselbeck was at his best. He set a club record for highest single-season passer rating (98.2). Named the NFC Pro Bowl starter after he tossed 24 touchdowns with just 9 interceptions, Hasselbeck had his best season when the Seahawks finished 13-3 to win their second straight division title.

From sixth-rounder to All-Pro. From backup to starter. And it was all started by the most unlikely motivational talk given by a leper in Jamaica—a man who has never watched a pro football game.

"It's been an amazing journey," Hasselbeck says.

DAVE DOWNING AND SHANNON DUNN-DOWNING

OLYMPIC SNOWBOARDERS

As in many good homes, God, faith and family are central in the lives of the Downing house-hold. What makes the Downings unique is the other common passion they share: snowboarding!

Though she has retired from the sport to be a full-time mom, Shannon Dunn-Downing is a women's snowboarding pioneer. After winning the bronze medal at snowboarding's Olympic debut at the 1998 Winter Games in Nagano, Japan, she went on to place fifth in the 2002 Winter Olympics in Salt Lake City, Utah.

Shannon was the first woman to perform several unique tricks in the U-shaped Halfpipe event, before winning Halfpipe championships at the Winter X Games, the International Ski Federation World Cup, the USSA Grand Prix and the U.S. Open. During the 1990s, she helped design and market snowboards and other action sports-wear for Burton Snowboards, a world-renowned snowboarding firm.

Dave Downing, a world-class snowboarder in his own right, assists Burton Snowboards with marketing clothing and acces-sories for action sports such as snowboarding, skating and surf-ing. Over the years, Dave has worked with Standard Films, which makes snowboard and motocross movies. He travels around the world and appears in films and documentaries to help promote the sport. In addition, he has appeared on the program *Firsthand*, a television series airing on Fuel TV, the worldwide, 24-hour chan-nel based in Australia, that is devoted to action sports.

Still, there's so much more to the Downings than snowboard-ing. True, they're totally into the sport they've revolutionized, but in recent years they've taken on a new challenge: being a Christian family with the values Jesus taught. As they raise their two sons, Doug and Shannon are finding that seeking intimacy with the Lord and living life His way bring more satisfaction than any earthly honors and awards ever could.

TRIPLE THREAT

By Amy Hammond Hagberg

For a long time, Dave and Shannon Downing's lives were all about snowboarding. Then God brought them together and gave them a new winning combination.

Dave Downing loves boards—on the snow or in the water. He spent his early years gearing up for a career as a professional surfer.

Then he discovered another kind of board—a snowboard.

David Dawson Downing, otherwise known as Triple D, is one of the most versatile snowboarders in the world. Highly respected in the industry, the spokesperson for Burton snowboards has been named one of the Top 20 snowboarders in the world.

His snowboarding videos are acknowledged for both their awe-inspiring scenery and his technical prowess. Adept at riding rails, halfpipes and jumps, Dave is perhaps best known for his skill on the rugged terrain of the wilderness. To him, snowboarding in the backcountry is exhilarating and challenging—he makes plunging off a 100-foot cliff look like a trip down a bunny hill.

But things have changed in the last few years, and Downing is now facing his greatest challenge yet: parenthood. Dave and his wife, two-time Olympic snowboarder Shannon Dunn-Downing, have two boys, Logan and Dillon, and those little guys have the Downing household spinning.

Shannon had a storybook career that may never be matched in the sport of women's snowboarding. One of the sport's most influential riders, Shannon was a serious competitor. A pro snowboarder since 1988, the Queen of the Halfpipe enjoyed extensive experience on the winner's podium.

Standing just 5' 2", this diminutive powerhouse represented the United States in two Olympics and brought home a bronze medal in the Halfpipe from the 1998 Games in Nagano, Japan. Shannon was also a familiar face at the X Games, accumulating four medals there, including gold in the Superpipe.

In addition, she starred in various snowboarding videos, and she works with the design team at Burton snowboards. At the core of this marriage of two snowboard superstars is something that might be somewhat unexpected in the world of halfpipes and ollies: faith.

Both Dave and Shannon are born-again Christians. Even though Dave's family regularly attended church while he was growing up, it wasn't until he went to a Christian Bible camp that he understood what faith is really all about.

"I found there that I can have a personal relationship with Jesus. I believed in God and I understood Jesus, but I didn't really make the connection. The church I went to, I kind of got turned off because there were so many regimens going on that I didn't understand. Once I found out that it was a personal thing, then I took Jesus as my Savior and really became a Christian," he says.

Dave's trust in God goes beyond the spiritual. To him, it even affects his assessment of his skills. "I'm amazed that I can even snowboard at all," he says. "I have no idea what I'm doing! It's all Him. Every day I go out and buckle on my snowboard, and He has complete control. He's riding the powder; He's doing the tricks. It's not me. What happens is just amazing."

Shannon went to a parochial school for most of her childhood. Even though she didn't go to church most Sundays, she took religion seriously. She prayed every night and was sincere, but she, like Dave, had never learned about a personal connection with Jesus.

Like so many young people, when Shannon got to college she explored other philosophies, including various New Age religions. Admittedly, her faith in God was just a "mishmash" of a variety of belief systems.

During her time spent attending college (which was extended because of her snowboarding), she continued checking out various faiths. Late in her college career, following a conversation with a friend, Shannon was driven to say this prayer: "God, could You please tell me who You are? I know You can do that because You're God. I need to know who You are, starting right now."

She also prayed that God would reveal to her the husband He had chosen for her. Just a month later, she met Dave in Italy while he was there for a photo shoot.

"He really helped me so much," Shannon says. "He got me a Bible because I told him I really wanted one, and we started going to church together. I understand now how being a Christian really affects others because Dave wasn't preachy or judgmental. He wouldn't talk about his faith unless I asked him. He changed me."

One day there was an altar call at the church they were attending, and Shannon trusted Christ. "I'm a whole different person—I'm like born-again, new, fresh."

Dave and Shannon were married in 1999. When their firstborn, Logan, was born, they made a monumental decision: Shannon would leave the world of competitive snowboarding to concentrate on raising their children. "I had snowboarded for nearly 14 years, and I had already done it all. I traveled all over the world and had the craziest schedule for years and years. It was like if I win another contest, I don't care. For my kids, I was totally ready to drop everything that I had done.

"It's like a 180 in the other direction," Shannon continues. "My life before was very spontaneous, just anything goes as far as when you do it, where you want to go. And I don't want to be like that now. I enjoy being home—there's nowhere I want to go."

She hasn't regretted it for a moment. "It's good, because I feel like we have a happy, healthy home right now."

Having children has an impact on the lives of all parents, but for the Downings the change in their lifestyle has been dramatic. Because so much of his career involves shooting snowboarding videos on virgin terrain, Dave has to travel extensively to remote locations throughout Canada, Europe and New Zealand to find the right shot. And many of these trips can last for weeks at a time.

"When you travel to a new spot, it takes you a few weeks to even find the good location that you want to film at," he says.

Now that he's the father of two, however, Dave tries to avoid those extended trips. "I don't go to places just to check out and hang out at until the snow gets good. I watch the weather and make sure it's good before I leave the family."

And when he does leave them, he's glad when he's headed back home. "My favorite part of being a family man is having something solid to come home to and be a part of. When I used to travel all year snowboarding, I never felt like I had a home. But now I really love home and can't wait to get back."

Shannon says it's hard on her and the boys when Dave is away. "He definitely travels quite a bit, but it depends on the season. It's okay for a couple of days, but Dave's last trip was 16 days, and that was just too long. But when he's home, he's totally home—so that's good."

Maintaining balance and consistency in their family life is a priority for the Downings, especially when it comes to raising their sons with a firm foundation in faith. And to do that, they make an effort to put God in the driver's seat.

"We have God at the center of our marriage, and that's how we want it. We can encourage each other and really just fellowship with each other because of our faith in Christ," says Dave. "I think Shannon and I try to let the Holy Spirit work in our lives. We try to read the Bible and pray together. I think trying to do what the Holy Spirit wants us to do instead of what we want to do is the thing to strive for."

The dynamic of their marriage and family and the way it all works together is amazing to Shannon. "It's just the bond that you share and just the love—the love your kids have for you and you have for them. Your marriage gets stronger and deeper; it's pretty cool. Sometimes love is not easy, you know—it can be taxing and sacrificial."

But it appears to be worth it. Parenting, of course, has its challenges, and for Shannon, one of those is finding ways to relate to her kids. "You just want to be the best mom you can, and at times I feel like I don't know how to do that. I think that's the biggest challenge—relating to your kids in the best way you can. They have emotions and you have emotions; they have their needs and you have your needs."

While Shannon's greatest challenge is fulfilling the needs of her children, her husband and herself, for Dave the biggest challenge is keeping Satan as far away from him and his family as possible. He realizes that as believers, they are always targets. A consistent prayer life is the key ingredient to keeping the enemy at bay.

As many families can attest, Christian families face a myriad of struggles in today's culture. "I think America is a very 'me, me' society. It's hard to get out of that. So just involving God in what we do is the key thing," says Dave.

Probably the biggest struggle for most modern families is a shortage of time, particularly time spent with God and centered in Christ. "You just get into what your kids are doing or you just get tired because you have tons on your plate," says Shannon.

Finding time for God is a real discipline, and having been a professional athlete has proven to be a great training ground in that regard for Shannon. "It's helpful to have been in sports to see how discipline really affects your performance. Well, it's the same with your walk. I often start out saying, 'I'm tired, I don't want to do this, I don't want to read my Bible.' Sometimes I just want to veg in front of the TV. But it's like sports—when you start working out, you say, 'Oh, this feels good; I feel so much better. How could I have not done this?'"

One of Shannon's favorite verses is Proverbs 3:6: "In all your ways acknowledge Him, and He will make your paths straight." It illustrates her walk with God and how she feels about success in life, both on and off the snow. The same principle applies to her role as a mother. "When I put God first and really study the Bible and pray, it makes a huge difference. My emotions are more even, and I can handle more in the day. I can just be a better mom and a better wife."

For the Downings, raising two boys in this complex world can be more challenging than the most complicated snowboarding feats. While they're doing their best, they realize that they don't have the same control that they do in sports.

"There's a serious 'X factor' involved—you don't know how your kids are going to wake up in the morning," says Shannon. "In sports, I felt like I had total control. I could practice and I could spend all the time, and I knew that if I did my homework the best result would happen. This parenting thing is totally different. It totally pushes you as a person. It is the ultimate learning experience."

Dave is still active in the snowboarding scene, especially in the free-riding area and big mountain riding. Shannon snowboards, too, but now just for fun. Even little Logan has been on a board—maybe someday we'll see him or his baby brother, Dillon, on the winner's podium. Yet whatever happens, it's clear that this is one family with the right priorities.

LAURIE BROWER

PRO GOLFER

Former LPGA golfer Laurie Brower is a survivor. At age two, she was run over by a car. At age nine, she had to swim to shore after a plane she was in crashed into the ocean. In 1989, she lost her mother, Dorothy, to cancer. And right now, she herself is winning a battle against cancer.

Born in Long Beach, California, Brower began her LPGA career in 1992 and competed throughout the 1990s. Her best Tour finish occurred in 1997 when she tied for third at the Standard Register PING. The year before, she notched a fourth-place finish at the Youngstown-Warren LPGA Classic, where she recorded her career-best round of 65.

In April 2000, Brower discovered a lump in her breast. While that one turned out to be benign, further tests revealed a second spot that was cancerous. Fortunately, the tumor was discovered in a very early stage and was removed; and Brower recently celebrated five years of being cancer-free.

Brower returned to the LPGA Tour in 2001, but retired from professional golf a year later, after suffering from Carpal Tunnel Syndrome and four broken bones in her foot.

Brower now spends her time on the front lines helping raise funds to combat the disease that took her mother's life and threatened her own. She is chairperson of the Lubbock, Texas, annual Susan G. Komen Breast Cancer Foundation's Swing for a Cure event, which has raised tens of thousands of dollars over the years and features other LPGA players who take part in the event.

A teaching pro at Hillcrest Country Club in Lubbock, Brower also plays the piano and is a volunteer coach for girls' golf at Lubbock high schools, but if you think that's all there is to Laurie Brower, think again. A woman of compassion, she took time out from pursuing her dreams to follow God's will for her life. A woman of strength, she found her way back from grief—and onto the green again. A woman of faith, she now sees that her detour was actually the path leading her to her true destiny—life in Jesus Christ.

PLAYING THROUGH

By Scott Bordow

Laurie Brower never won an event on the LPGA Tour, but she has already proved that she's a winner.

Laurie Brower has been run over by a car, suffered a wrist injury that threatened her career, and spent two and half years taking care of her dying mother. So what's the big deal if a four-foot putt for par slides past the hole?

"I'm not Laurie Brower the golfer," she says, "I'm Laurie Brower. I'm pretty much one of those people whose attitude doesn't fluctuate over a good score or a bad score."

Brower was one of those LPGA pros you never hear about—the ones who struggle to make a living, who cut costs by sharing a room at the local Motel 6 and frequent Denny's for their Grand Slam breakfasts.

In some ways, though, Brower's story is more remarkable than that of any woman who displays silver chalices on her mantle or boasts a seven-figure savings account. It's a story that transcends the ups and downs of professional golf.

Laurie Brower began to discover how tough life can be when she was a rambunctious toddler growing up in Southern California. She crawled out of her car seat one day and accidentally put the automobile in gear. Then she fell out the car door and was run over. The back tire rolled right across her diaper.

Amazingly, the doctors who examined Laurie could find little wrong with her. For the next six weeks, though, she rarely stopped crying, and she couldn't suck her thumb. A subsequent visit to the doctor revealed why: She had broken both arms.

"They finally figured it out," she says.

Things settled down until 1986 when Brower, by then a Southern California junior champ and two-time Southwest Conference Player of the Year at Texas Tech, decided to try the LPGA's qualifying school. She had graduated from Tech in 1985 with a degree in handicap recreation, and she felt ready for the pros. She was on her way to making the Tour when she hit a routine fairway shot—and her wrist screamed in pain.

"I said, 'Wow! That hurt!'" Brower recalls.

Brower had ripped all the cartilage in her wrist. For the next several months, her wrist was so sore she couldn't pick up a pencil. X-rays showed that the bones in the wrist had fused together. Following surgery, one doctor told Laurie she would never play golf again.

Brower still isn't sure if the wrist injury was a result of her wanderlust as a toddler. "How would you know?" she asks.

For the next 18 months, Brower rehabilitated her wrist, hoping to give pro golf another shot. Just as she began to get ready to go back on the Tour, her father called, asking whether she could come home. Her mom was dying of a brain tumor.

All her life, Brower had waited for the opportunity to prove she could play with the best golfers in the world. She had overcome any lingering effects of the car accident. She had recovered from the wrist injury. This was her time to shine.

But when her dad called, she didn't give golf a second thought. "My dad asked me to quit work. I did," Brower says. "I never asked why. It was my mother."

Nor did Gary Brower think twice about asking his daughter to suspend her career. He knew Laurie had always put others before herself.

When she was seven years old, for example, she would take get-well cards to older neighbors who were ill. "I don't know how she got the cards," Gary says. "But she'd take them to the people, help around the house and try to cheer them up."

"That's just Laurie," Gary says of his daughter's gracious attitude.

For 30 months in the late 1980s, Brower took care of her mom, never straying far from home. Laurie wanted to be there when Mrs. Brower needed help.

Some days were good. During those times, Dorothy Brower was lucid, could hold a conversation and remember life as it once was. Other days were worse, when Mrs. Brower's brain would be "foggy," as Brower describes it.

"When she woke up from naps, she would scream with fear if nobody was there," Brower says. "So I tried to stay close by. I was there whenever anything bad happened."

The only respite for Brower was *Late Night with David Letterman*. After Dorothy went to bed, Brower would turn on the television and try to remember that there was light in all the darkness. "David Letterman was the only thing that would make me laugh," she said. "The stupid pet tricks, stupid human tricks. It felt wonderful just to laugh."

Brower knew she was losing potentially the best years of her golf career, but she didn't care. Taking care of her mom was more important.

Even though her mind and body were failing, Laurie's mom insisted that her daughter not give up on her future. So Laurie bought a net to hit balls into and some Astroturf to putt on. The backyard became her field of dreams. "I couldn't leave her. That's how I practiced," she says.

"I was very thankful for that time with my mom," Brower says. "Otherwise I wouldn't have been home with her and gotten to spend so much quality time. I wouldn't change any of it. None of it. I had to watch her deteriorate, but God took her in a very gentle way, and I was there for her."

Dorothy died in 1989.

Says Gary of Laurie's dedication to her mom, "It set Laurie back quite a bit, but she's the kind of gal who doesn't let things get her down. She's always optimistic."

There was a time when Brower might have felt sorry for herself, felt that life had given her a raw deal. But that all changed in January 1992 when Brower accepted Jesus Christ as her personal Savior.

It wasn't a decision born from one significant moment. Rather, it was a gradual process, one that had begun in a seemingly mundane way.

Brower was rehabilitating her wrist in her doctor's office when she noticed one of the therapists wearing a pin that said, "Happy Birthday, Jesus."

"I said, 'I don't get it,'" Brower recalls.

Brower wasn't a stranger to Christianity. Her mom was a believer. So was her brother. And nearly every member of the Texas Tech women's golf team confessed their faith in Christ.

Brower just didn't want to hear any of it.

"I didn't really care what they were or who they were," she says. "I just wanted them to leave me alone. I wanted to be an individual."

There was something about the therapist, though, that intrigued her. The two talked, and Brower agreed to read Josh McDowell's book *More Than a Carpenter*. "A few months later, it all made sense," she says. "It's been the toughest thing I've ever done. And," she quickly adds, "the most rewarding."

Brower's faith has helped her cope with her mother's death. Laurie knows now that God had a plan for her life—and if taking care of her mother was part of that plan, she should accept it with grace.

"I've never talked much about it, but there's no question I have a pretty strong faith inside," she says.

After her mom died, Brower wasn't emotionally ready to tee it up full-time, so she wandered. She worked a couple of odd jobs, one as a secretary for a pet-supply distributor, another at Yorba Linda Country Club in California and a third at Anaheim Stadium making popcorn.

"She's very work-oriented," Gary says. "She had to stop making popcorn because she was getting it all over the place. She just made too much."

Of course, there were the fringe benefits. "She got to watch a lot of baseball," Gary says. "She's a big Angels fan."

Brower wasn't sure what direction her future was heading. Then Barb Mucha, a close friend who played on the Tour at that time, asked Brower if she wouldn't mind caddying for her in some West Coast tournaments.

Brower immediately said yes. What else did she have to do?

One of Brower's employers—she won't say who—told her, "You might as well go ahead. It's as close as you'll ever get to playing on the Tour." Brower could have been angry. But she recognized there was some truth in the statement. "I wasn't playing, and I thought, *Well, maybe he's right.*"

He wasn't.

Brower got a call from a friend asking her to play in a mini-tour event in Southern California. Brower said thanks, but no thanks. She still wasn't emotionally ready. The friend insisted. Brower said yes, and then changed her mind. "That's fine," the friend said, "but you better find somebody to pick me up at the airport."

The next morning, Brower met her friend for breakfast. The two began to talk, and the mini-tour event in Victorville, California, was the prime topic.

Finally, Brower agreed to play.

She nearly regretted the decision. She stepped up to the tee at the first hole and suddenly realized it was the same course where her mom had last watched her play. Brower started sobbing. She took a nine and headed for the second hole, certain she wouldn't be able to finish.

"Then I realized my mom wouldn't want to see me like this," she says.

Brower rallied to shoot a 75. She finished fifth, earning $900. Pocket change on the LPGA Tour, but the money wasn't important. The fire was back. "It was time to get the ball rolling," she decided.

Less than a year later, she had proved her boss wrong. She made the Tour in October 1991.

Brower played on the Tour throughout the 1990s and into the new millennium. She never won a tournament, but she's okay with that.

"Everything's in perspective," she says. "I look at my mom's situation and I think, 'Well, at least I'm alive.' That keeps you pretty calm."

DENNIS BYRD

NFL DEFENSIVE END

"In a New York minute, everything can change," Don Henley once sang.[1] Sadly, everything changed in an instant for New York Jets rising star defensive end Dennis Byrd following a collision with teammate Scott Mersereau on November 29, 1992.

At that time, the collision left Byrd with a broken neck—he was paralyzed from the waist down. A nation wondered if he'd ever walk again. Well, thanks to surgery, rehabilitation, hard work and determination—and let's not forget, Byrd's unshakable faith—he did.

Byrd walks with a limp. He has limited balance and stamina, but he refuses to use a wheelchair. He continues to partake in a rehabilitation program—something he'll likely have to work at harder as he gets older.

The Jets have named an award after him: the Dennis Byrd Award, given each year to the club's most inspirational teammate. Byrd, however, stays away from accolades. He lives a quiet life in Oklahoma with his wife, Angela, and their four children.

Is Byrd at peace with the way things have turned out? Probably to the surprise of many, the answer is yes. Why? Because Byrd has an unshakeable faith in God. He knows without a doubt that it was Jesus who saw him through his darkest hour—and Jesus who continues to use his story to inspire others. By walking in faith, Byrd has been able to be open to whatever God might be calling him to do with his life.

Recently, Byrd has been serving as an assistant football coach at Lincoln Christian School in Tulsa, Oklahoma, coaching the defensive line. The school's football stadium, Dennis Byrd Stadium, is named after him.

Inducted into the University of Tulsa's Athletic Hall of Fame in 2005, Byrd also does charity work (he heads the Dennis Byrd Foundation), and is an accomplished sculptor. During 2006, Byrd was featured on ESPN's "Outside the Lines."

FOREVER FRIENDS

By Dave Branon

Dennis Byrd faced paralysis and a shattered career, but found his wife, Angela, ready to help him put the pieces back together.

The hit was one of those bone-jarring football scenes that makes you turn away from the TV replay. Like the shot of Joe Theismann's broken leg several years ago. Or Mike Utley's unusual head-over-heels fall in 1991.

Football is a game of crushing collisions, but you never grow accustomed to seeing a player take a hit that you know could do permanent damage. As another physical tragedy unfolds before your eyes, a somber pall is cast over the game. What had been so absolutely essential seconds before—the score, the down, the strategy—all becomes incidental.

Suddenly you are reminded that players have lives off the field, and that what just happened could change one life forever. Instantly, concerns for family, friends and feelings replace our strong interest in fans, football and fame.

So it was with the hit Dennis Byrd took on November 29, 1992. When Kansas City Chief quarterback Dave Krieg sidestepped Byrd, the Jets defensive end barreled headfirst into teammate Scott Mersereau, who was coming after Krieg from the other side. Despite a lifetime of training in the proper way to take a hit, Byrd had no time to prepare himself for this collision. He instinctively ducked his head just before he slammed into Mersereau.

Stunned by the violent hit, Mersereau fell to the turf—the wind knocked out of him. Within seconds, though, he was back on his feet.

Not so with Byrd. He knew almost immediately how seriously he had been hurt. "I started to get up and the only thing that moved was my neck," he recalls. "My head came off the ground and I felt something crack or crunch, so I put my neck back down. Then the next thing I tried to do was pick my feet up."

But he couldn't. As he lay in front of the stunned stadium crowd and as team personnel scurried to attend to him, Byrd realized what was wrong. "Kyle Clifton stood over me," Byrd relates, "and he asked me if I was okay and said, 'Get up.' I told him I had broken my neck and was paralyzed."

Clifton, a 6' 4" linebacker, knelt down beside his teammate, took Byrd's hand and cried. Byrd recalls, "That's a picture that sticks in my mind, how he was just crushed."

And so was the rest of the team as their fellow warrior was gingerly eased onto a cart with team trainer Pepper Burruss's hands clasped firmly around Byrd's helmeted head to immobilize it. He maintained that position from that moment on the field until Byrd was in the hospital.

Nothing has been the same for Dennis Byrd since that collision. Instantly, he was transformed from a finely tuned, hard-bodied professional football player who could run the 40 in 4.78 seconds into a helpless hospital patient who had to have everything done for him. He could no longer hug his wife, Angela, or pick up his daughter, Ashton. He was paralyzed.

The week leading up to this fateful game at Giants Stadium had been full of the kinds of quiet joys that were characteristic of the Byrd household—events that now seem more significant than Dennis and Angela could have ever expected.

On Monday, Dennis bought his daughter a toy doctor's kit.

On Wednesday, the Byrds discovered that Angie was pregnant with their second child.

Also on Wednesday, the Byrds met for a Bible study during which the topic of discussion was a paralytic man who was healed when Peter told him to get up and walk in the name of Jesus Christ.

On Thursday, which was Thanksgiving, the Byrds and some friends watched the Detroit Lions play the Dallas Cowboys, a game that was preceded by a special feature on Mike Utley, the Lions' paralyzed teammate.

On Sunday, Dennis Byrd found himself in Lenox Hill Hospital in Manhattan, thinking a million thoughts about how utterly and drastically everything had changed.

Later he would equate what had happened to him to something that happened to a man whose life story is retold for us in the Bible. "Job was a man of faith," Byrd explains. "And a lot of things came against Job. His faith was tried, and he tried to [see if he could] be broken, but he wouldn't turn his face [away from] God. I feel much the same way. I mean, how would you try to take the faith away from somebody who was an athlete, that loved what he did? You'd paralyze him and take away everything that he loved so much, and attack his physical life and his family life."

An injury like this can destroy families. It can turn a unified group of people who love each other and who together share the day-to-day joys and struggles of life into estranged individuals who hardly know each other.

Dennis Byrd was afraid that might happen to him.

Two weeks after the injury, Byrd's neck had been stabilized by surgery, and he was ready to begin rehabilitation. Still paralyzed, he knew he was facing a long, grueling ordeal as he fought to get back on his feet. And his caretakers knew he needed to be moved to a hospital that specializes in rehab.

Mount Sinai Medical Center in the Upper East Side of Manhattan was chosen as his next home. After his first day of tedious therapy in this new location, the exhausted former football player lay on his back, contemplating his situation. "I was being stripped down to my essence," he recalls about this day in his book *Rise and Walk*, "with no such thing as privacy, no such thing as pride in the sense I'd felt it before. I was just a body. I was still Dennis Byrd, but this body that contained me was something different now."

It was on this night that he came face to face with the kinds of questions that must confront everyone who has been touched by a life-changing illness or injury. Questions like: *How do the significant people in my life perceive me now? Do I still have value to them even though I am not whole? Am I too big a burden for them to carry?*

"I could handle feeling pathetic," Byrd recalls as he thinks about that night. "I was truly prepared to handle anything, with the help of Jesus Christ. But Angela, why should she have to deal with this, maybe for the rest of her life? I was determined to walk again. I had no doubt I would. But what if I was wrong? What if the Lord had other plans for me? What if I'd never rise out of a wheelchair? I knew I could live with that, but could Angela?"

When Angela came to visit that night, Byrd told her what he was thinking. "It's not fair for you to have to be with me like this forever," he told her. "It's not fair for you to have to take care of me like this. I'd understand if you wanted to leave me."

Angela Byrd was astonished at what she was hearing. Tears came to her eyes as she bent over her husband. "Dennis, I can't believe you'd say that. I can't believe you'd even think of that." She reached across that hospital bed and hugged her helpless man. Together they cried as she held him, and he knew that he would never again have to fear losing his companion.

One night some time later, as the two were lying in bed together, Angela noticed that she could hear his heart beating. "Dennis, that sounds so good."

"What?" he asked.

"Just hearing your heart beat."

During an interview with Diane Sawyer of the ABC-TV newsmagazine *Prime Time Live*, Angela said, "It didn't matter what kind of shape he left [the hospital in], as long as he was alive."

More than a year had passed since that moment of truth. Dennis Byrd thrilled a watching world by regaining his ability to walk, and he has even confessed to jogging a few yards at the family home in Oklahoma.

True, Byrd has been separated from one of his loves in life: football. "It hurts a whole lot," he says in describing what he has lost in not being able to suit up for the Jets anymore. "You can't replace it. I just keep hanging on to the memories."

But there are other loves that his injury cannot take away. Like his love for Jesus Christ. As he began the long road to recovery, he faced the kind of crisis that would make some people doubt God's presence. Yet Byrd says, "I was in a halo brace with tubes coming out of my body. I couldn't move. Jesus Christ was with me more than ever. He gave me strength. It was an opportunity to turn my back or to use the things I've learned all my life." He used his knowledge of God then, and he continues to do so today.

And his love for his family remains a continual source of help. "My wife loves me for who I am, not what I am," he has discovered.

The results of that brutal hit that no one cares to see again have brought to Dennis Byrd a fame that he could never have achieved by simply being a talented defensive end. "I certainly don't remember being this good a football player to have this much attention," he said while still on the mend in New York City.

Byrd's own sense of purpose has been solidified by what has transpired. "I know why it was me," he says. "The strength I have inside, I know I can get through this. I'm glad it was me and not someone else."

Note

1. Don Henley, "New York Minute," © Donald Hugh Henley, WB Music Corporation, Los Angeles, CA. All rights reserved.

PAYNE STEWART

GOLF LEGEND

The putt only covered 15 feet, but it seemed more like 100 to the gallery gathered at the eighteenth hole at Pinehurst No. 2 on that early Sunday evening in June 1999. It traveled uphill, broke ever so slightly to the right . . . and slipped gently into the cup.

Payne Stewart, wearing his trademark knickers and argyle socks, hoisted the ball up to the heavens. The crowd roared. And for the second time in his career, Stewart was crowned champion of the U.S. Open—the most prestigious event for American golfers.

The victory would be his last on the PGA Tour.

Four months later, on October 25, 1999, Payne Stewart entered the gates of heaven after his private jet plowed into a dirt field in Minot, South Dakota, taking the lives of Stewart and three business associates. His death at only 42 years old shook the golf world and the entire nation.

Stewart was a bona fide golf superstar, one of the tiny handful of competitors who made young Tiger Woods very nervous out on the links. Stewart had won 3 majors—including the U.S. Open—and 11 PGA events overall. But his passing meant more than the loss of an amazing golfer—the game had also lost one of its most fun-loving and colorful, yet sensitive and caring, individuals.

The world paid tribute to Stewart at a memorial service a few days after his death. Some 3,000 people attended, including more than 100 PGA tour officials, and players such as Jack Nicklaus, Greg Norman, Tiger Woods, David Duval, Davis Love III and Phil Mickelson, whom Stewart had beaten by just one stroke to win the Open.

Before Stewart's death, he and his wife, Tracey, had founded the Payne Stewart Family Foundation, which financially supports charities that help underprivileged children and families. In addition to his wife, Stewart was survived by his daughter, Chelsea, and son, Aaron.

In 2000, Tracey Stewart teamed up with Ken Abraham to write the *New York Times* best-selling book *Payne Stewart: The Authorized Biography*. That same year, the PGA Tour Policy Board created The

Payne Stewart Award, given annually to a PGA golfer who shares Payne's respect for the traditions of the game, as well as for upholding golf's longtime commitment to charitable causes.

In 2001, Stewart was posthumously inducted into the World Golf Hall of Fame, but his greatest honor, he would have said, was being inducted into the Kingdom. He wasn't a Bible thumper—he preached the good news of salvation through the quiet transformation of his personal and professional life. Little signs made clear the great change that had occurred in his soul, as he sought, in his final months, to be the husband, the father and the golfer God had called him to be.

TRANSFORMATION

By Art Stricklin

Chronicling the spiritual journey of Payne Stewart

To understand golfer Payne Stewart—the most public of sports figures, who died the most public of deaths in October 1999—you have to look deeper to see what changed him over the last 18 months of his life. And the best way to do that is through the eyes of his friends and colleagues.

"The one thing I think about Payne was that he was genuine," says fellow PGA pro David Ogrin.

Ogrin knew Stewart from his college days when David played for Texas A&M and Payne starred for the Southern Methodist University Mustangs. He observed him closely for nearly 20 years and is perhaps one of the best qualified to comment on Stewart's decade-long journey from a highly successful yet highly dissatisfied pro golfer to a confident and peaceful believer in Jesus Christ in the last year and a half of his life.

"I knew him when he was the perfect Frat Rat," Ogrin says. "I played against him for three years and knew he was a genuine hard worker. At times he could be a genuine pain in the neck, but we all knew he was a genuine champion. When he talked to you, he was genuinely interested in what you had to say."

But Ogrin, like Stewart's many close friends, including golfer Paul Azinger, sports agent Robert Fraley and former star pitcher Orel Hershiser, came to see a genuine difference in the once egotistical and often sarcastic golfer.

"In the last couple of years, Payne became a genuine Christian. He had earned everything a man could earn on his own in the golf world and found that it wasn't enough," Ogrin adds. "To understand what finished out the man and the grasp that it held on him, you have to see what Jesus has to offer and the place He played in Payne's life."

The difference, according to PGA Tour chaplain Larry Moody, was that Stewart went from having a religion he could fall back on if needed, to a personal relationship with Jesus, which carried him through the highs and lows of his final months on this bunker we call Earth.

Moody began making the rounds on the PGA Tour in 1981, Stewart's rookie year. He, too, witnessed firsthand the changes in Stewart's life. "We had some good talks after his father passed away in the early 1990s. Then his good friend Paul Azinger was stricken with cancer in 1993. He had talked to Payne about not being in the land of the living and going to the land of the dying, but actually being in the land of the dying and heading for the land of the living.

"Although Paul was sure where he was going, Payne did not share the same confidence," Moody adds.

All the while, Stewart's agent Fraley and his wife, Dixie, along with good friend Van Ardan, were continually talking to him about a relationship with Jesus and how the peace and joy of a personal Savior far outstripped any golf honors Stewart would ever win.

The most constant reminder of his need to change inside and out came from his two young children, Chelsea and Aaron. They began attending a Christian sports camp each summer in Missouri, Stewart's home state, and they made sure of their eternal destiny during one of the camps.

"We always said they were raising Payne just like he was raising them," Stewart's longtime golf teacher Chuck Cook says. "They brought home the Christian life and the Christian values to him on a daily basis."

When it came time for Tracey and Payne to select a school for the two kids, the Stewarts sought out one of the top Christian schools near their Orlando, Florida, home, the First Academy at the First Baptist Church of Orlando.

While the denominational label was ultimately unimportant, the teaching Payne received at the church proved to be one of the final mileposts of his spiritual journey. Stewart began attending a men's Bible study led by Hershiser, who also stressed the need for a personal relationship with God. Orel emphasized that being accepted by God is not based on good works but on faith in Jesus—the One who had paid the penalty for his sins and could make him righteous before a holy God.

"God used a little bit of everybody in Payne's life," says former First Baptist associate pastor J. B. Collingsworth. "Larry Moody and Paul Azinger were factors, his kids brought it home to him daily, and he came to First Baptist Orlando, where he joined the men's Bible study and learned many things here."

Stewart also became good friends with the late Byron Nelson, a golfing legend and one of the game's greatest winners, who once told Payne of his own need to have Jesus in his life to help, guide and comfort him.

Despite all the shared knowledge and friendly persuasion, Stewart had to settle his spiritual relationship alone, which he did—asking Christ into his life as his personal Savior and Lord privately in 1998.

Shortly after that, Payne's son, Aaron, helped Dad let the world in on his changed life. Early in the 1999 golf season, Aaron gave his dad his WWJD bracelet, which stands for "What Would Jesus Do?" The youngster proved wise beyond his years when he challenged Dad to come out of the closet and let others know about his private commitment to Christ.

Moody was one of the first to hear from Payne about his bold commitment when he encountered him on the practice range at the Shell Houston Open in April 1999. Seeing Stewart wearing the bracelet, Moody asked for some background information and listened as Stewart told him that God had truly changed his mind, body and spirit.

"In the last year, I knew Payne was committed to God, but in Houston was when I found he was unashamed publicly of his commitment," Moody says.

The rest of the sports world caught on a few months later when Stewart conquered the demanding Pinehurst No. 2 layout to win his second U.S. Open title, capping the victory with a bracelet-encircled fist thrust into the air on the eighteenth green. That photo and Stewart's spoken, public commitment were played around the world the following day as his path from carnal, clutter-filled darkness to peaceful life became clear.

Collingsworth, who became a friend of Stewart's, spoke with Stewart at a post-U.S. Open party thrown in July 1999 by his wife to help map out his future path. "He told me he wasn't going to be a 'Bible thumper'; that wasn't his style. But he wanted everybody to know it was Jesus, Jesus, Jesus who had done this great thing in his life, and that was all-important."

Moody said that in the past Stewart would have mocked players who attended the weekly Bible study for being less than perfect and even quite human at times. "I told him only sinners came to the Bible study, and if he wasn't one, then he shouldn't show up because he would make the rest of us look bad," Moody says, recalling his tongue-in-check response.

Eventually, of course, Stewart became aware that although he was less than perfect as a player or a person, he was forgiven by the One whom he had accepted into his life.

For Darin Hoff, who grew up with Stewart in Springfield, Missouri, and who had known Payne since age 15, the change began to come into focus when his buddy lost the U.S. Open title to Lee Janzen in 1998. "I saw he was truly gracious in defeat and really cheered Lee Janzen when he won. I knew that was not like the old

Payne. His faith was so much more important to him than it ever had been before," Hoff says.

Hoff was working as an assistant golf pro in South Bend, Indiana, when he received the stunning news of the death of Stewart. Payne's old friend grabbed a flight to Orlando for the memorial service. He spent much of the trip thinking about his friend and the difference he had seen in his life over the last year.

"At the memorial service, I realized I didn't have what Payne did. It was like God was standing right there calling me to come to Him. My life was changed forever on that day, and I know I will never be the same."

Collingsworth says that in the months just after Stewart's death, he heard from people all over the country who had been affected by it and desired to follow the golfer's spiritual path.

Moody, who has dealt with professional golfers for two decades, can only shake his head in amazement at the pathway Stewart traveled in his professional, private and spiritual life. "What a tremendous legacy he has left us. How thrilled we are to know him and to know that his story is attracting so many others to what Payne found."

It was a winding pathway, but an eternally fulfilling one for the most public of golfers, who made the most public of life-changing commitments. And now all the world is finding out about the transformation that made Payne Stewart's life—and death—a tribute to His Savior.

DAVE DRAVECKY

MAJOR LEAGUE PITCHER

No one who saw it, either in person or on television, will ever forget it. It's summer 1989. A major league pitcher winds up and hurls the ball toward the plate—something he has done thousands of times before. Only this time a loud *crack!* rings out and the pitcher crumples to the ground in agony, his humerus bone shattered. For Dave Dravecky the tragedy was double, in that he had just pitched his first game after cancer surgery on his arm. His comeback had ended.

In all, Dave Dravecky pitched seven major league seasons with the San Diego Padres and the San Francisco Giants. The left-hander compiled a solid 64-57 career record and a 3.13 earned run average, pitching in the National League Championship Series in 1984 and 1987 along the way, as well as in the 1984 World Series between the Padres and the Detroit Tigers. Dravecky's career post-season ERA (0.35 in 25.7 innings) and hits allowed per nine innings (4.21) remain among some of the best numbers ever recorded in major league history.

However, baseball and sports fans the world over recall the tremendous courage and steadfastness Dravecky displayed through the late 1980s when he was diagnosed with a cancerous desmoid tumor in his pitching arm. When his arm shattered on that fateful August day in 1989, it signaled that the cancer had returned. Eventually the arm had to be amputated in order to prevent the cancer from spreading—and to save his life.

Though those were dark days for Dave and his wife, Jan, they came out of the experience with renewed faith and with hope for the future. While leaving baseball behind wasn't easy for Dave, he was able to move forward as he learned to trust that the Creator had a plan—that God was in control of his life.

Following His leading, Dravecky and his wife founded the Outreach of Hope, based in Colorado Springs, an organization that gives encouragement to others who have either been stricken with cancer, are suffering a serious illness or have undergone an amputation. In addition to their charitable work, the Draveckys are highly sought-after motivational speakers. Together they have authored several inspirational books, and Dave has written two himself, on the topic of baseball.

WHEN THE CHEERING STOPS

By Gari Meacham

*Former pro athlete Dave Dravecky and his wife
talk about life after the games end.*

Making it to the big leagues is tough. Staying there is even tougher.

Yet there is another season in a ballplayer's life—one that seldom gets noticed but one that descends on him like an unexpected curveball. It's the season of retirement.

The adoring crowds are no longer cheering. Autograph seekers don't chase them, and the competition and team play that were once a daily routine are now only a fond memory. An empty silence prevails as the former star settles into life beyond the intensity of pro ball.

The path to retirement is unique for each player, yet the common thread that bonds former prospects or stars of the past is pain. The pain of walking away from a game that's been a part of their life since childhood. The pain of accepting themselves when no one around them is cheering. And finally, the pain of discovering who they are and what talent they possess outside of throwing a ball and handling a bat.

Pitching a baseball was all former San Francisco Giant Dave Dravecky ever wanted to do. He did it well, and his talent led him to an All-Star game in 1983, plus successful outings in postseason play in 1984 and 1987. Dravecky's story is well-known: a cancerous lump removed from his pitching arm in 1988; a miraculous comeback leading to a start for the Giants on August 10, 1989; the sound of his pitching arm snapping on a delivery to the Expos Tim Raines; and the painful amputation of that arm because the cancer just wouldn't go away.

Dave and Jan Dravecky were thrown into a furious cycle of fear, anger and depression. Retirement meant not only giving up baseball but also handling the reality of cancer and amputation.

"When baseball was over and my arm was gone, I looked in the mirror and said, 'What's left?' My whole foundation crumbled, and I realized that even my relationship with God was based on performance. I felt I had to perform well to please Him," says Dravecky. "When my tools for performance and security were gone, my internal struggle began to rage in the form of anger and depression. But God used that time in my life to make me real. Everyone looked at me as a hero, but a hero's shoes are impossible to fill. God has taught me to believe what I preach—to trust in the One who is in control."

As Dave struggled through his life-changing circumstances, his wife, Jan, was battling her own problems. "I spent a full year in depression," explains Jan. "I had been told that depression contradicted my belief in God and showed a lack of faith on my part. I didn't know how to handle my fear of the future or Dave's rage at being forced into an arena he didn't want to be in. A wise counselor began to address my pain by showing me the truth about my life and the depression I felt. Slowly, the truth began to set me free."

The Draveckys's journey toward contentment has been an intense pursuit to strip away the images so easily maintained in the glitter and hype of pro baseball. "God has changed my heart in so many ways," reflects Dave. "I used to be so black and white about things. I left no room for gray areas or imperfections in others. I feel as if I'm more tolerant and vulnerable now, even with my children. I feel a confidence and contentment in the role God has me in."

Dave and Jan now spend their time encouraging others through their Outreach of Hope ministry and by fulfilling a busy speaking engagement schedule that takes Dave to cities throughout the country. "It feels good to be real," says Dave. "I've learned the value of communicating, and I long to be transparent for God's glory."

The Draveckys's pain and experiences after baseball have been widely publicized—and certainly Dave represents a majority of ballplayers who gave their hearts to the game, only to walk away and start a new life facing great obstacles. But for all the pain that retirement may bring, every man who steps onto the diamond in the big league uniform knows he wouldn't trade his memories for anything.

With the support of family and friends, the athlete can eventually smile at the future and enjoy his life, knowing that every young phenom who crushes the ball at the plate or throws blazing strikes to the batter will one day have to retire too. It's part of the game. And like any good baseball game, the applause and drive toward victory ends in the ninth inning. Win or lose, you pack up your belongings and go home.

MIKE SINGLETARY

NFL HALL OF FAMER

They already knew of Mike Singletary, linebacker extraordinaire, in
and around Chicago prior to 1985.
But the entire nation arguably met
Singletary for the first time—rapping, no less—when the Super Bowl-
bound Bears recorded "The Super
Bowl Shuffle": "I'm Samurai Mike,
I stop 'em cold/Part of the defense,
big and bold."[1]

Wrapping up—not rapping—opposing ball carriers was
Singletary's forte during a 12-year NFL career highlighted by 10
straight Pro Bowl appearances (the most ever by a Chicago Bear),
a Super Bowl championship (1985) and selection to the Pro Football Hall of Fame in 1998. Then in 1999, he was named to the
Sporting News list of 100 Greatest Football Players (Singletary was
ranked number 56).

A tireless worker who during his playing days prepared for games
with the thoroughness of a coach, Singletary actually became an
NFL coach in 2003, joining the Baltimore Ravens as a linebackers
coach. He has since moved on to San Francisco, where he serves as
the team's assistant head coach/defense. Many believe it's only a
matter of time before Singletary becomes a head coach.

As far as Singletary is concerned, he already has it all: a relationship with Jesus Christ, a solid marriage with his wife, and seven
beautiful kids. He is eager to share with the world (and has already
done so in three books and countless guest speaking engagements)
what the Lord has done in his life. And with his eyes fixed on Jesus,
Singletary has no doubt that the future will bring even more amazing blessings!

BEAR WITH ME

By Mike Sandrolini

Mike Singletary let his playing career end, but he and his wife, Kim, fought hard to make sure their marriage didn't.

Before he took the field for his final NFL season in 1992, Mike Singletary set some goals for himself. They were no different from the ones he had established every season since he joined the Bears in 1981: Be the best player he could possibly be and help his team be the best they could be.

"It's important to set our sights on something," says Singletary. "I worked my tail off before the start of the season. I didn't want to go out sitting on the back of a convertible, waving my hand, and saying, 'Wasn't I good!' I wanted to leave this game at my best."

True to form, Singletary retired at the top of his game—despite the Bears' dismal 5-11 season. Neither his playing time nor the quality of his play diminished as the frustrating year wore on. In fact, Singletary started every game in 1992 and led the Bears in tackles—the eleventh straight season he finished either first or second on the team in that category. And in his last game at Soldier Field, Singletary led the Bears to an emotional upset of the tough Pittsburgh Steelers.

Mike Singletary has been living up to his own great expectations for a long time. During his illustrious 12-year career, Singletary was named to the NFC Pro Bowl team 10 times; selected NFL Defensive Player of the Year twice; named twice as UPI's NFC Defensive Player of the Year; and received NFL Man of the Year honors in 1990 for his on-field play and off-the-field humanitarian contributions.

Singletary's days of accumulating football awards may be over, but his commitment to excellence is not. His desire to be the best is still as much a part of him as his trademark bulging eyes.

That burning desire carries over to the Singletary household, where Mike takes great pride in being the best husband he can be for his wife, Kim. But that ambition—like his on-field fire—is not new. Just as Singletary worked hard in training camp to ensure his success on the gridiron during the season, so Mike and Kim have put in the effort to make Team Singletary work every day. Communication, they say, is number one on a short list of keys to a successful marriage. But both believe that factors besides lack of communication have contributed to rampant divorce rates in the United States.

"One of the biggest reasons that marriages are falling apart," Mike says, "is because of the family breakdown before marriage. In the last 20 years, husbands and wives have come from broken homes. So you don't really know how to be a husband or how to be a wife. Eventually, you end up falling into the same trap."

Singletary himself, the youngest of 10 children, is the product of a broken home. As a youngster, he observed a father whose pattern of behavior would one day affect his relationship with Kim. Singletary's parents divorced when he was 12. His father was a preacher at a small church in Houston, where he grew up.

"I'm a Christian man saying this, but I really feel that when my mom and dad got married at 15 and 16, they did not have any idea what it took," he says. "They weren't there for each other. It just did not work.

"Under normal circumstances, what I have seen failed marriages do to children is to create a guilt feeling. I know in my brothers and sisters it definitely did create a sense of 'Who am I?' A loss of commitment. Denial. I think it gives a kid his first reason to say, 'Hey, if it doesn't work out, bail out. Who cares? That's the way life is.'"

The Singletarys are living proof that life does not have to be that way. They showed that a marriage can survive tough times if a husband and wife are willing to face the problem and do what's necessary to resolve it.

Mike and Kim Singletary were married in May 1984. Several months into their marriage, however, Mike was feeling anything but marital bliss. "I had gotten to a point in my life where I was really frustrated," Singletary recalls. "I said, 'Lord, what's going on here? I'm making good money, and I have a lot of notoriety. What's up? I'm getting to a point where I don't think You're up there. What's going on?'"

"The Lord spoke to me just about as clear as I'd be talking to you," Singletary says. "He said, 'If you really, really want to be used by Me, you've gotta clean up your act.'"

"I said, 'Wait a minute. Clean up what act?'"

"He said, 'Well, you've got a problem with your father. Have you forgiven him?'"

"'Well, wait a minute. Why do we have to talk about that?'"

"'Because that's part of it.'"

Singletary felt hatred and bitterness toward his father for leaving him, his mother, his brothers and his sisters to marry another woman. But he wanted to do the best thing, so he finally got on the horn with his father. "One day I called my dad, and he and I talked for about two and a half hours," Singletary says. "We cried; we yelled at each other and everything else, but we got it straight."

Reconciling with his father turned out to be the easy part.

"After that, God said, 'Now, step two. You need to come clean with Kim.'" God was prodding Mike to tell Kim that he had not been faithful to her during their engagement.

"'Wait a minute.' I protested. 'This was before we got married. That's between You and me.'"

"'No, not for you it isn't.'"

"I know the Lord knew that telling Him about it wasn't enough," Singletary says. "He needed to break me, and that's what it was going to take. I had to come clean with my wife and say, 'Honey, you know all the time we were dating or engaged, I wasn't faithful to you.'"

It took some time and many sleepless nights for Singletary to finally tell Kim. He realized that confessing his unfaithfulness would hurt her and possibly run the risk of ruining their marriage. But not telling her, he says, would have been worse. "I realized I had a choice," Singletary stated in his book *Singletary on Singletary*. "I could continue to live a lie, live with deceit and live with guilt.

I could make a lot of money from my profession, acquire a lot of possessions, buy my wife clothes and jewelry and anything else she might like. I could have children, dress them nice, send them to good schools and watch them grow without imparting any wisdom. I could have everything this life had to offer except peace and a clear conscience."

While Kim and Mike were vacationing alone on a Caribbean island, he finally told her his secret. "That was the hardest thing I've ever had to do," Singletary says. "She was hurt."

As hard as it was on Mike, it must have been worse for Kim, yet she remembers his pain as much as hers. "Initially, I felt sorry for him," she recalls, "because I could see for a couple of months that he wasn't sleeping. He wasn't relaxed ever, and I could see he was really struggling with something. By the time he got it out, it had been really painful for him, and I kind of felt bad for him. I knew he was repentant and remorseful, and I concentrated my focus on him. But later it seemed that he got better and I got angry."

"Even before that time, there was kind of a subconscious mistrust of him," she explains. "If he told me, 'I'll be home at 8 o'clock,' I never could put all the eggs in that basket. I'd say, 'Well, I'll give it to 9:30, and then we'll see from there.' I hadn't had a lot of faith and trust in him, and then when he told me, it wasn't so shocking. I remember feeling very embarrassed, feeling that everybody we knew at Baylor University probably knew about this. I figured everybody looked at me as, 'What a fool! How could you not know this was going on?'"

For Singletary, the weeks and months following his confession were the most painful in their marriage. Their bond of trust had been violated. Kim says she considered a separation "because I was so angry at the time," but she never followed through on it. Divorce never entered her mind.

Working through the anger and developing a sense of trust again took time. "It took about a year to get past that," Singletary says. "A year and a half for her to be healed from it and to trust me again."

"He explained to me that I could do 10 times more than what he has done, and I still wouldn't know the hurt he was feeling," Kim says. "The trust had to grow, and there was kind of a time of proving himself. As hard as I could, I tried not to hang things over his head."

How did Mike win back Kim's trust?

"She knows beyond a shadow of a doubt that I had really given my life to Jesus Christ," he says, "and I was going to be a man of faith. I tell her to this day, I say, 'Sweetheart, I want you to understand something: I'm not going to fail you if I don't fail God. My eyes are on Him, and I've got to do the things that are right in His eyes. If I can please Him, then I know I won't have a problem pleasing you.'"

"I don't know at what point I trusted him again," Kim adds, "but I trust him completely now."

Making a conscious choice to forgive Mike also played a big part in helping Kim get over her hurt and anger—and in putting their marriage back together.

"I knew spiritually how unforgiveness would bind me, for I knew people who had hate and bitterness in their lives, and how it physically, mentally and emotionally ruins you," she says. "I grew up in a Christian home, and that foundation was laid. God forgave me and forgiveness was in my nature. I knew I had to come to the point that I forgave him."

Kim says their marriage has been strengthened because of what they went through. "I can't believe how the Lord has used it. Even in our own families, there have been times when we could advise others because we've been there. Mike finally arrived at where he was intended to be spiritually, where God wanted him to be as a man, as a leader and as a public figure in this country. And I realized that my walk with God doesn't go through anybody else. It goes straight to the Lord."

Kim believes Mike did the right thing by telling her about his conduct during their engagement. She says having secrets in a marriage is "unhealthy."

"I'm very grateful," she says, referring to how things worked out with her and Mike. "Having secrets in a marriage is so binding. I'm very glad it's all behind us. If I see an old friend from Baylor, Mike doesn't have to pass out thinking, *Oh, no.*"

Mike Singletary knows he did the right thing, too. "It took some time and some faith, but the Lord took us through it," he says. "Man, I'll tell you—what a change! The walk of faith changed my life, and the Lord used me and worked in my life as never before."

Now, with a clear conscience and an upfront relationship, Mike Singletary knows that nothing can keep him from being the best husband he can possibly be.

Note
1. Lloyd Barry, Bobby Daniels, Richard Meyer and Melvin Barton Owens, Jr., "The Superbowl Shuffle," © 2004 MPI Home Video.

SUE SEMRAU

COLLEGE BASKETBALL COACH

In the world of sports, one often hears about players who go the extra mile to succeed. Meet Sue Semrau, a coach who operates in that same mind-set.

As head coach of the Seminoles, Florida State University women's basketball team, Semrau wanted the general public to get a firsthand look at her top-notch squad and help her pay tribute to the team's senior class. So, prior to their final 2005-2006 regular season home game, Semrau waged her Tent for Tickets campaign, literally camping outside of the Donald L. Tucker Center for two days and nights, selling tickets to the game! Semrau exceeded her goal of selling 3,000 tickets, as nearly 4,000 fans showed up to root for the Seminoles on game day. And the women didn't disappoint: They outscored nationally ranked Boston College.

The Seminoles have gained quite a bit of national recognition under Semrau, who completed her tenth season at FSU in 2007. She has won more games than any other women's basketball coach in school history, was twice named Atlantic Coast Conference Coach of the Year, guided the Seminoles to consecutive 20-win seasons and appearances in the NCAA tournaments of 2004-05 and 2005-06, and advanced her team to postseason play during four straight years.

Off the court, Semrau actively volunteers with the Fellowship of Christian Athletes and speaks to community and alumni groups around the state. In addition, she has participated in the Athletes in Action Basketball Coaches Clinic, which annually features many top coaches and teachers of the game.

Through good seasons and bad, wins and losses, Semrau knows that God's hand is guiding her, bringing her to where she needs to be, giving her strength to do what needs to be done. She trusts in Him to create the game plan—her job is just to show up for the game!

LETTING GO

By Jim Crosby

In the face of tragedy, Sue Semrau and her Florida State ladies basketball team found out that only in recognizing that they weren't in control could they reach their potential.

The phone call came at 3 A.M. A groggy Sue Semrau answered, trying to focus her mind on what she was hearing and not the drowsiness that lingered on. "Coach, I have some bad news. They took Ronalda to the hospital and she didn't make it," said her roommate, Florida State guard Alicia Gladden.

How could this be, Coach Semrau wondered? She had just seen the Seminoles 6′ 5″ post player from Ashburn, Georgia, a few hours earlier. Ronalda Pierce was animated, happy and full of life as she participated in an off-season pickup game at the basketball training center. Now, without warning, she was gone—the victim of an aneurysm on June 8, 2004.

How are we going to recover from this? How will we ever handle this and bounce back? thought Semrau as she pondered all that had happened to the Florida State women's basketball team. One year earlier another death had stunned the program when beloved academic advisor Matthew Schmauch died unexpectedly from an allergic reaction to nuts. In May 2004, starting center Genesis Choice had decided to forgo her senior season. Yet even more bad news was on its way. In August, another key member of the squad told the team she was pregnant and would not play. "I was on vacation when I got that news, and I read the entire book of Job," says Semrau.

Now, as the Seminoles headed into what many believed would be a make-or-break season for Semrau and her staff, they would face it without the top six scorers from 2003-04. Hired in 1997 to rebuild Florida State's women's basketball team, Semrau had enjoyed only two winning seasons up to that point.

However, Semrau's faith did not waver. Despite the record, the coach believed she was accomplishing what she set out to do. She felt that God had put her at FSU to build a nationally recognized program, despite the degree of difficulty involved.

Athletics director Dave Hart was aware of how hard that job would be when he hired her. "Sue probably inherited the worst women's basketball program in the country. Certainly one in turmoil," says Hart. "I thought it would take a person of boundless energy and a positive outlook to get our program headed in the right direction."

In light of all the adversity, the lifting had turned into heavy lifting. Semrau realized it was out of her hands. "Honestly, it was at that point that I realized it was going to be God's strength that was the only thing that would pull us through. That was what I really started praying for," she says.

She began reading Ephesians 3:16-21 over and over. She drew special strength from the verses that said, "Now to him who is able to do immeasurably more than all we ask or imagine, according to his power that is at work within us, to him be glory" (vv. 20-21).

It was time to reemphasize to the team the quote on their locker room wall: "Coming together is a beginning. Keeping together is progress. Working together is success." If only the remaining 10 players would buy into that. It was their only chance.

Before the adversity hit, Sue had settled on a new approach that had impressed Dave Hart. "When Sue and I sat down to have our regularly scheduled end-of-the-year evaluation, she had a very specific plan in mind. She was going to delegate more. It's easy to say that, but when you are used to being 'hands on' it is difficult to do."

Semrau brought in Cori Close as associate head coach from UC Santa Barbara. Close had been a member of the UCLA staff in the 1990s. She would join Angie Johnson (Louisville), a longtime assistant with Semrau, and Lance White (Texas Tech). Semrau now felt her staff was "equally yoked" in faith and philosophy.

Close became Sue's offensive coordinator and White was the defensive coordinator. "That's something I used from Coach [Bobby] Bowden's philosophy. He has been such a tremendous mentor to me. To have an offensive and defensive coordinator and to give Angie the authority of being the recruiting coordinator, they could all play off each other," says Semrau.

The coaches loved the system. "It freed each of us to work within our giftedness a little better," says Close, who admits the roles were more like that of offensive and defensive planners.

The plan was in place, but how would the badly shaken team respond? Coach Sue saw her mission coming into sharper focus. "I think I have the opportunity to have a ministry with a leather ball and a hardwood court that's rare. St. Francis of Assisi said it best: 'Preach the gospel always and when necessary use words.'" As Semrau thought about this, she decided, "We had to intentionally head into the pain instead of running from it. I'm proud of the way our players responded to that."

While the skeptics wondered if FSU would even win a game in the tough ACC, Coach Johnson says, "Whenever you have such adversity and have to pull a team together, it has to come from the leadership. We had to be able to pull upon Sue's lead to be a single voice that told them, 'Despite what has happened, you can still achieve the goals we set out.'"

After winning their 2004-05 season opener, the Seminoles headed to Gainesville to play the Florida Gators, a team they had not beaten in 13 years. An amazing transformation occurred that night. FSU roared out to a 24-point halftime lead over the heavily favored Gators and ended up with a 72-62 victory.

"We felt that God was saying, 'I'm going to strip you of everything you think you need and watch what I do,'" said Johnson. "Just like he told Gideon he needed only 300 men to defeat the Midianite army, God said to us, 'I'm going to do it with a bunch of ragamuffins, and it is going to be total commitment to each other, and it is going to be all about team,' and He built it."

After that November night, the Seminoles went on a spectacular run. As the skeptics watched transfixed, the team ran off 12 straight victories—ringing in the New Year with a 13-1 mark. "Our goal had been to win 21 games, finish in the top four in the ACC and reach the NCAA tournament," says Close. What had seemed like a pipe dream didn't seem unreachable anymore.

After reaching mid-January at 15-2, their stamina was really tested. On January 16, the Seminoles were down by 12 points to Maryland in the second half but rallied behind senior Roneeka Hodges's 39 points to force an overtime and win 95-91. Afterward, Semrau reflected, "I can't say enough about this team and their never-say-die attitude. They find a way to step in and get it done."

Four days later against North Carolina (14-2), the Seminoles took it into overtime and won again, 79-73. Then, on January 24 they traveled to Virginia Tech, where they came from behind and won again—this time in double overtime.

Three overtimes in a row. Three wins! The ragamuffins had sole possession of first place in the ACC. "Winning those overtime games made a statement about the team's character," says Dave Hart. "I've been around athletics all my life, and I've never seen a team display more mental toughness than our women's basketball team did. That includes all sports."

The critics had disappeared. The Seminole bandwagon had become a big one. As always, Semrau remained focused and unruffled by wins or losses. Even in the worst of times she had not worried if she was in the right place. "God is very clear. Every time He has asked me to move on, I have sensed in my spirit pretty clear direction," she says. Semrau knew her work was not finished at Florida State.

Now a confident Seminole squad was undaunted by any deficit. At Wake Forest they trailed by 10 points with 3:43 left and pulled out a 71-69 victory. Then came a triple overtime victory against Virginia Tech.

The Seminoles would go on to achieve every one of their goals. They finished 24-8 and fourth in the ACC—and they earned a trip to the NCAA tournament, where they defeated Richmond before losing to the defending champions, Connecticut.

Florida State had made believers out of everyone. Before the season the Seminoles had been fearfully asking, "What's next, Lord?" in anticipation of the next catastrophe. At season's end the same question was joyfully being asked because they couldn't wait for the next good thing to happen.

"I think I realized that God's blessing is not in what we human beings always think is good. His blessing can also be a difficult thing for us. I feel we were all blessed with an inner strength that maybe we never would have developed without those circumstances," says Semrau.

In athletics, coaches always stress the importance of team play and trusting each other. Sue Semrau was able to get her team to buy into that concept totally. "She's just a good person. You love to see good things happen to good people and that's what occurred for our women this past basketball season. I include the entire staff and team in that statement, but specifically Sue Semrau," says A. D. Hart.

When it was all over, Coach Semrau remembered a significant postgame occurrence from February 19, after FSU's triple overtime win. "Ronalda's family was there. Her mother, Linda, came up to me and said that was the greatest game she had ever seen. Then she asked, 'Do you know how many minutes it took you to win? It took 55 minutes.'" Fifty-five was Ronalda's number. The team had worn it on their sneakers all year.

"You kind of think Ronalda was up there saying, 'We'll get this done, but it's going to take 55 minutes to do it,'" Semrau says.

On February 23, the team had an open date. It was Ronalda's birthday. They celebrated her life by telling stories, laughing and crying, while eating her favorite Red Velvet Cake. It was then they realized that this togetherness, this closeness as a team, was Ronalda's parting gift to them.

The Seminoles also received another gift during those turbulent times: hope. Sue Semrau looked past difficult circumstances and trusted God to bring her team through a desert of misfortune. She proved that coaching isn't always Xs and Os—often, guidance and leadership come into play. Coach Sue has learned to rely on and trust in the guidance of Christ, who has never failed her.

THANKS

The 1980s is commonly known as the decade of greed, but in my life, it turned out to be the decade of growth—spiritual growth, that is.

Back then, I attended a Catholic church in Lostant, a small north-central Illinois town some 15 miles due south of Peru on U.S. Route 51. No, not the country Peru—it's my hometown, situated between the Illinois River and Interstate 80.

Whenever the church's pastor, Ron Roth, spoke from the pulpit, I noticed I didn't fidget in the pew, nod off, tune him out . . . or keep looking at my watch, wondering how long until the opening kickoff of the Chicago Bears game. Ron drove home Christian and spiritual principles not with fire, brimstone and guilt, but with humorous anecdotes and a catchy phrase that's stuck with me to this day: "God loves you, He really does!"

I remember listening to an audiocassette tape of one of Ron's messages—mind you, CDs had not yet been invented—in which he said (I'm paraphrasing here) that God speaks to us in thoughts, hunches and ideas. "If God ever spoke to me in an audible voice," Ron said, "I would die of cardiac arrest!"

Around three years ago, I happened to be wise enough to act on what, I believe, was one of those God-inspired hunches. Thus, I want to give credit where credit is due. My first thank-you is to God. He gave me the idea for this book.

Thanks also to:

Robert Walker and Dave Branon, *Sports Spectrum* magazine's publisher and managing editor, respectively. Robert said, "Let's go for it" when I presented the project to him, and has been a calm and steady influence throughout. Dave, an accomplished author himself, offered advice and guidance—and patience—whenever I peppered him with questions about books and publishing (which was often).

Debbie Miller and Laurie Nelson of the *Sports Spectrum* staff. Whenever I needed a contact's e-mail address or phone number, or back issues of *Sports Spectrum*, Debbie and Laurie went out of their way to help and always came through in the clutch.

Steve Lawson, senior editor at Regal Books. Steve took an immediate interest in this project when I discussed it with him at a publishing conference, and his expertise helped mold it into what you now hold in your hands.

Jason Bachman, Charlene Baumbich, Dave Jarvis, Joe Maxwell and Lanny Slevin. I have been blessed with their many years of friendship, and each was particularly encouraging throughout the process of putting this book together.

The *Sports Spectrum* writers whose stories appear in these pages. These talented men and women are some of the best in the business.

Besides all of the above, countless individuals have either answered questions, helped me line up photographs or have provided me with information on the various personalities featured on these pages. Among those who have been especially helpful: Dana Ashley of the Pujols Family Foundation; Katie Bredemeier of the Luis Palau Association; Deborah Carrillo with the PGA Tour Creative and Photographic Services; staff from The Gary Carter Foundation; John George of Getty Images; Connie Hemmer with Dave Dravecky's Outreach of Hope; Paul Hickey of the Detroit Shock; Marci Moran Pritts of Kurt Warner's First Things First Foundation; Michael Suttle, who assists Mary Lou Retton; Tina Thomas of the Florida State University Athletic Department; and Trish Wingerson of the Orlando Magic.

I am indebted to you all.

Mike Sandrolini

ABOUT SPORTS SPECTRUM

Sports Spectrum Magazine is published six times per year by Sports Spectrum Publishing, P.O. Box 2037, Indian Trail, North Carolina, 28079-2037. Each colorful issue profiles sports' biggest names taking their game—and their faith—to the next level.

In addition, *Sports Spectrum* delivers regular features that will help you become the best you can be, on and off the field. Keep one step ahead of the competition with helpful tips from athletic trainers and coaches. Learn how to maintain and improve your physical wellbeing. Grow spiritually by participating in the magazine's "Power Up" series and by reading other features that address Christian values and biblical principles. To subscribe, call toll free: 1-866-821-2971.

Sports Spectrum also is only a mouse click away. Log on to www.sportsspectrum.com and get everything you need to stay on top of the sports world. The website's signature feature "The Daily" provides scores, current news and trivia, along with an inside look on a featured athlete.

On the road or at home, tune into Sports Spectrum Radio each Saturday at noon Eastern time for insightful interviews with sports stars of today . . . and yesterday. The weekly half-hour show is broadcast by approximately 258 stations throughout the United States, Puerto Rico, Samoa and the Canadian province of Ontario.

ABOUT THE COMPILER

Mike Sandrolini has worked for more than 20 years as a professional writer, editor, reporter and columnist with four newspapers (daily and weekly) and one magazine publishing company. He has also been involved in Christian publishing as a reporter and writer since the early 1990s, including work for *Sports Spectrum* Magazine. He has been published in Sharing the Victory, the official magazine of the  Fellowship of Christian Athletes; Breakaway and Charisma; SLAM; Basketball Digest; and Preview Sports. Other venues for his work include the Chicago Tribune, Daily Herald, Copley Newspapers, Liberty Suburban Chicago newspapers and the Chicago Bear Report. His work has been recognized in various state and national newspaper editorial excellence contests.

Go One-on-One with Sports Legends

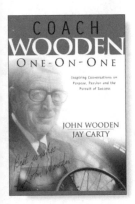

**Coach Wooden
One-on-One**
Inspiring Conversations on
Purpose, Passion and the
Pursuit of Success
John Wooden and *Jay Carty*
ISBN 978.08307.32913

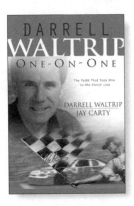

**Darrell Waltrip
One-on-One**
The Faith That Took Him
to the Finish Line
Darrell Waltrip and *Jay Carty*
ISBN 978.08307.34634

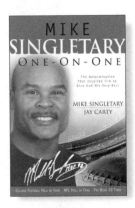

**Mike Singletary
One-on-One**
The Determination That Inspired
Him to Give God His Very Best
Mike Singletary and *Jay Carty*
ISBN 978.08307.37024

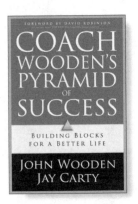

Coach Wooden's Pyramid of Success
Building Blocks for a Better Life
John Wooden and *Jay Carty*
ISBN 978.08307.36799

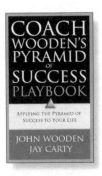

**Coach Wooden's Pyramid
of Success Playbook**
Applying the Pyramid of Success to Your Life
John Wooden and *Jay Carty*
ISBN 978.08307.37932